P 3

LEISURE IN ART AND LITERATURE

WARWICK STUDIES IN THE EUROPEAN HUMANITIES

General Editor: Michael Mallett, Professor of History, University of Warwick.

This series is designed for publications deriving from the European Humanities Research Centre at the University of Warwick, which was founded to promote interdisciplinary and comparative research in the European Humanities. The Centre's aims, pursued through research projects, conferences, seminars and visiting fellowships, result in this series of publications.

Nicholas Hewitt (*editor*)
THE CULTURE OF RECONSTRUCTION

J. R. Mulryne and Margaret Shewring (*editors*)
WAR, LITERATURE AND THE ARTS IN SIXTEENTH-CENTURY EUROPE
THEATRE OF THE ENGLISH AND ITALIAN RENAISSANCE

Brian Rigby and Nicholas Hewitt (*editors*)
FRANCE AND THE MASS MEDIA

Margaret Tudeau-Clayton and Martin Warner (*editors*)
ADDRESSING FRANK KERMODE: ESSAYS IN CRITICISM AND INTERPRETATION

Tom Winnifrith and Cyril Barrett (*editors*)
THE PHILOSOPHY OF LEISURE
LEISURE IN ART AND LITERATURE

Tom Winnifrith (*editor*)
PERSPECTIVES ON ALBANIA

Leisure in Art and Literature

Edited by

Tom Winnifrith

Chairman, Department of English and Comparative Literary Studies
University of Warwick

Cyril Barrett

Reader in Philosophy
University of Warwick

M

First published 1992

Published by
MACMILLAN ACADEMIC AND PROFESSIONAL LTD
Houndmills, Basingstoke, Hampshire RG21 2XS
and London
Companies and representatives
throughout the world

Printed in Hong Kong

ISBN 0–333–51874–8

A catalogue record for this book is
available from the British Library

Contents

vi   *Contents*

List of Illustrations

List of Illustrations

Preface

The papers in this volume were delivered at a conference on leisure in art and literature held at the University of Warwick on 4-5 June 1988. As with all such conferences to which the contributors are not personally invited (for the simple reason that in a research project such as this it is unlikely to be known in advance who might be interested in the subject or what their particular interests are) the result is a somewhat unstructured collection, but not necessarily any the worse for that. It can have a refreshing informality, and emphases can emerge unexpectedly. This is what happened with the Warwick conference. A strong emphasis was placed on leisure as described in the classics, and its effect on the British educational system. This latter element in the book links it with the previous volume on the philosophy of leisure, in so far as papers on education deal with the use made of games in the moral formation of children. In this volume, however, a precise connection is made between games and classical literature.

Acknowledgements

The plates in this book are reproduced by courtesy of the following institutions: plate 1 – the Tate Gallery; plates 2, 7, 8 and 10 – the British Museum; plate 3 – the Walker Art Gallery; plate 4 – the Dulwich Picture Library; plate 5 – the Shakespeare Memorial Theatre Art Gallery; plate 6 – the Guildhall Art Gallery; plate 9 is from the editor's collection.

Dr J. A. Morgan's chapter 'Edwardian Oxbridge' is an expanded version of a paper previously published in *Victorian Studies* in the Autumn of 1991.

In preparing the manuscript the editors would like to gratefully acknowledge the help of Mrs C. A. Cave, Mrs M. Franklin and Mrs H. Winnifrith.

Notes on the Contributors

Cyril Barrett is Reader in Philosophy at the University of Warwick and coeditor with Dr Winnifrith of *The Philosophy of Leisure*. He has edited and written books on aesthetics, including Wittgenstein's lectures on aesthetics, and *Op Art*.

John Bromhead has been Assistant Librarian at the University of Birmingham from 1961 and was previously with Shropshire County Library. He has been in charge of the National Centre for Athletics Literature since 1971.

G. M. Hyde is Lecturer in English and Comparative Literature at the University of East Anglia. He was Reader in Contemporary English Literature at Marie Curie University, Lublin, Poland from 1976 to 1979. His publications include work on literary theory and modernism, translations of Russian and Polish texts, a study of the novels of Vladimir Nabokov, 1977, and two books on D. H. Lawrence, 1981 and 1990. He is currently writing a book on Russian Formalism.

S. J. S. Ickringill lectures in history at the University of Ulster. He is currently Chairman of the Irish Association for American Studies. He has written on the American Revolutionary Period as well as on sports and leisure topics.

Edward Larrissy is Lecturer in English and Comparative Literature at the University of Warwick and has written works on Blake and modern poetry.

J. A. Mangan is a Fellow of the Royal Historical Society and the Royal Anthropological Institute. He is also a member of the Academic Committee of the Imperial and Commonwealth Museum Trust, a founder member and Inaugural Chairman of the British Society of Sports History, and the founder and Senior Editor of the *British Journal of Sports History*. He is an authority on the nineteenth and twentieth century public school system, has published many articles on the subject and is the author of

Athleticism in the Victorian and Edwardian public school and *The games ethic and imperialism*.

Malcolm Tozer is Headmaster of Northamptonshire Grammar School. His research interests span the overlapping histories of education, sport and imperialism for the Victorian and Edwardian eras, and he has published his findings in a series of essays, lectures and books.

Shearer West is Lecturer in the History of Art of Leicester University. She has published articles in *Victorian Studies, British Journal for Eighteenth-Century Studies, Theatre Notebook, The Times Literary Supplement* and *Art History*. She is author of *The Image of the Actor: Verbal and Visual Representation in the Age of Garrick and Kemble* and *Chagall*. She is currently working on a major study of English portraiture and an exhibition on theatrical controversy for the 1993 Nottingham Festival.

Tom Winnifrith is Chairman of the English Department at the University of Warwick and was, for five years, Director of the European Humanities Research Centre. He has published books on the Brontës, the Balkans, George Orwell and leisure.

Introduction

Cyril Barrett

Given the theme of leisure in literature, art and education, the scope is limitless, not only in material but also in the aspects of the subject that can be covered. Most of these aspects have been just about touched on in one way or another.

The first thing to be noted is the obvious fact that art and literature are leisure activities themselves. And so is education. Indeed, the Greek word for leisure (*scholé*) is the root of 'school', 'scholar', 'scholastic' and other words connected with learning. School children and students, however unwillingly they go to their places of education, are a leisured class. Whether they are being prepared for the turmoil and stress of life or for a life of further leisure, they are temporarily free from the business of earning a living.

Writers, painters, composers, sculptors, actors, dancers and architects may think they are workers. They certainly work. But then work and leisure are not incompatible, as we argued in the previous volume. This is evident. Anglers toil with the rod and line; batsmen toil at the wicket; racing cyclists and long distance runners toil up hill and down dale. The fact that they are remunerated for what they do does not make their work any less a leisure activity. But even if we were to concede that a professional, a wage-earning actor or football player (both 'players') is, like a carpenter or plumber, not to be regarded as engaged in a leisure activity, for those for whom he is working his activity provides entertainment. For them his work is a source of leisure.

Leisure and leisure activities have not always been regarded as fit subjects for art and literature. At best their inclusion in the arts appears to be incidental and of no importance. They are mentioned or depicted simply because these are among the less unpleasant or less objectionable human activities; and since humans indulge in them, they cannot be ignored completely. So we have mention of or depictions of feasts, the playing of musical instruments, dancing and games in the earliest literature (including sacred books), murals (interiors of Egyptian tombs) and monuments. Indeed, if some

1

research student with no better or more ambitious topic (and an
abundance of time and resources at his or her disposal) were to
quantify the amount of space – inches of print, square inches or
metres of canvas or wall-space – that has been devoted to the
description and depiction of leisure activities the result might well
astound the high-minded. And what might amaze them still more
would be the accumulation of material as we advance into the
modern era (the last five centuries or so).

Their riposte might well be that this only shows how trivial and
degenerate the human race has become. Perhaps. If one takes a
high religious, moral, socially responsible and generally serious
attitude towards literature and art this might well be an arguable
case. It is a case that has been argued this way and that by
theologians, moralists and the socially conscious for a few millen-
nia. But what we are concerned with in this volume is not the use
to which literature and art can be *put* in the service of religion,
morality and social and political ends. Nor, on the other hand, do
we deny that some of the greatest art – the vast majority of it, if you
will – was produced in the service of religion, morality, social
reflection and other serious pursuits. But in reply to the objections
that (a) leisure is not a suitable subject for serious literature and art;
and (b) leisure is not, in itself, directly beneficial, morally or
religiously/spiritually or socially, we reply as follows.

First, the greatness of a work of art or of literature does not
reside in the seriousness of the subject *alone*. The reserves of
galleries and museums are piled high with serious works that no
one wishes to look at. Likewise secondhand book repositories are
stocked with serious books that no one wants to read. It is not the
seriousness of the subject that makes for great literature and art,
but the manner in which the subject matter is handled. What could
be more trivial than a kitchen table with a pitcher, a plate, a knife,
half a loaf and some fruit on it? Or a pair of old shoes? And yet they
are the subject matter of masterpieces by Chardin and Van Gogh.

This might be conceded – indeed, in any sane account of the
arts, would have to be conceded. But (it will be objected) to treat
leisure seriously is either to turn it into something else – a moral,
political, polemical or some other activity – or to make it utterly
ridiculous, like writing about the philosophy or psychology of
jokes. Leisure, so the argument goes, is *essentially* lighthearted,
relaxed and unserious. To treat it seriously is to turn it into
something else, something that, strictly speaking, is not leisure,

though it might have the appearance of leisure – sports, games and pastimes.

This is in itself serious as an objection. It is, however, based on a misconception (or, if one were to be more charitable, an alternative conception) of what leisure is. In the previous volume, I argued, following Aristotle, that leisure is the most serious human occupation or activity. As Aristotle put it, the gods do not concern themselves with such trivial occupations as negotiating, buying and selling, making contracts, litigation, politics, making war and all those activities that mortals take so seriously. Their concern is with contemplation and relaxation. More seriously, he argued that the most important human activity is the one which most differentiates humans from other animals. This, in his opinion, is the pursuit of knowledge, understanding and wisdom. These are all leisure activities. He placed moral behaviour and religious observance (in so far as he considered them at all) rather lower on the scale of human activity.

This, of course, is to invert the accepted wisdom of literary and art critics – music and dance critics may be more sympathetic. If it is true, then the case for taking leisure seriously as the subject matter of literature and art is enhanced. This is the second point. It becomes apparent as soon as we reflect on the literary position of Plato's *Symposium*, Boccaccio's *Decameron* and Chaucer's *Canterbury Tales*, all describing the leisure activities of conversation, learned discussion and story-telling. It would not seem too far-fetched to include all of Plato's dialogues and, indeed, all philosophical dialogues – Berkeley's and Hume's, for instance – within the ambit of intellectual recreation, the sort of leisure activity that, it is fondly hoped, flourishes in men's literary clubs such as the Savile, Garrick and Colony.

Indeed – and this is the third point – it could be argued that all art and literature, *in so far as it is art and literature*, is primarily a leisure activity. This, on the face of it, may seem to be hard to argue. What of sacred literature, statues, paintings and music; moral works; works of social, political and historical importance? They surely cannot be put on a par with sport, feasting, rambling or even entertaining conversation. There is something distasteful about treating the Bible 'as literature'. (Wittgenstein objected to it strongly.) Pope St Pius X in a *motu proprio* forbade the use of orchestral instruments during services in church because, when they were played, people went to church as to a concert. This is proper. But it is equally proper (or at least not improper) to perform Beethoven's Missa Solemnis or any other splendid Mass in a concert hall. Oratorios, the brain-child of St Philip Neri, were designed to entertain as well as instruct and were not necessarily performed in church. And, as for the Bible, there can hardly be anything improper in reading it for the beauty of its poetry (Psalms and The Song of Solomon) and of its narrative (Ruth, Esther, The Book of Job, etc.). This does not turn the sacred texts into mere entertainment. Nor do *Gulliver's Travels* or *Animal Farm* lose their satirical bite if read as entertaining narratives.

This point is made very forcefully by Shearer West in her paper on the eighteenth-century theatre in England. There were those who opposed any form of theatrical representation; those who defended tragedy on Aristotelian lines in that it inculcated and upheld moral values; and those who went to the theatre for fun, entertainment or a riotous time. For the latter the theatre was an occasion for recreation, relaxation and, hence, leisure. Of that there can be no question. Ironically, however, those who opposed theatrical representations, not excluding tragedy, emphasised the essentially recreational and, hence, the leisure element of all forms of theatrical performance. Moreover, they established its seriousness. It may seem paradoxical to describe the *Oresteia* or *Lear* as entertainment. But that is what they are. And the puritanical opponents of the theatre confirm this. How anyone can derive pleasure and satisfaction from watching the representation of the sufferings of others is a question to which Aristotle (presumably replying to Plato) addressed himself, and aestheticians and theorists of tragedy have been struggling with it ever since. But the fact that it is a *representation* and not reality places it in the class of trivial pursuits, along with conjuring, miming, charades and fancy dress, where, in one sense – namely, as a leisure activity – it rightfully belongs.

Now, if tragedy is a leisure activity, then leisure can concern itself with very serious matters: life and death, murder, revenge, betrayal, incest, adultery – all the evils flesh is heir to.

But we are concerned with the *portrayal* of leisure and not the leisure activity of portraying. Murder and treachery may be fit subjects for the leisure activity that is tragedy, but what we are concerned with is the portrayal of that leisure activity. Once again Dr West comes to our assistance with her illustrations of how tragedians and other actors and actresses were not only described

in literature but also portrayed in paint. Though Hogarth portrayed
the seamier side of the theatre (as well as the 'theatre of the seamy'
– *The Rake's Progress*) and Zoffany its lighter side, Reynolds, Gainsborough and other academicians portrayed its more serious side,
depicting such famous actors and actresses as Garrick, Kemble,
Kean and Mrs Siddons, not only in tragic roles, but also in heroic
poses characteristic of classical heroes, gods and goddesses (poses
originally borrowed from the theatre). As Dr West argues, this was
done, partly, to establish the seriousness of the theatre.

If the theatre, particularly tragic drama, can be a serious matter,
albeit a leisure activity, so too can the portrayal of what are usually
regarded as more trivial leisure pursuits such as games and sport.

This point is ably argued by Dr Winnifrith and John Bromhead,
and in a different context by Dr Tozer and Dr Mangan. Winnifrith
is one of the few commentators on Homer's presentation of the
funeral games in the *Iliad* (book 23) and Virgil's in the *Aeneid* (book
5). Most other commentators regard these passages in the epics as
rest passages between or prior to great martial events. The careful
– or even the cursory – reader must be aware that they are
anything but restful or idyllic. Indeed, in almost every event there
is nothing but strife and unpleasantness, not just competitiveness,
which is to be expected, but cheating, foul play, rancour, jealousy,
partisanship and hostility on the part of the spectators. Nothing
that happens at a present-day football game, tennis match, athletics meeting or cricket match is without its counterpart in the
funeral games described by Homer and Virgil. As Winnifrith
points out, the games get nastier under Virgil's pen, and reach the
stage of vileness equal to our own day, when they have ceased to
be leisure activities, under the pens of Statius and Silius Italicus.
(Ministers of sport please note.)

Thus, in the works of Homer and Virgil, sports – rowing,
running, boxing, chariot racing, archery, javelin throwing etc. –
are treated very seriously indeed. Though this may not be what
constitutes them as leisure activities, it is an indicator of the moral
worth and psychological character of those who partake in them.
This is inevitably so, and is true of every leisure activity, even of
such tranquil occupations as working on an allotment or knitting.
There is no leisure activity, however tranquil, that does not reflect
the human passions and moral dispositions of those who engage
in it, both honourable and dishonourable: ambition, zeal, envy,
sloth, dishonesty, fair play, hatred, selflessness, equanimity of

mind, boastfulness, contentiousness, guile, perseverance, etc., etc. Just as young cubs play out and thus develop the actions they will have to perform in their maturity, so humans behave in leisure as they do in the more serious affairs of life. And, after all, leisure is a form of life and, at the limit, spills into it. The difference between a wilful late tackle and an assault is very slight, and recently the authorities have taken cognisance of this.

Thus, sport and, indeed, most leisure activities are rich material for literature, drama, film and other performing arts. Winnifrith has shown how the moral element of sport can be woven into the very substance of epics, and in what manner – loosely (Homer); well, if thinly, (Virgil); crudely (Statius and Silius). The funeral games are not a restful interlude but an integral part of the *Iliad* and the *Aeneid*. They bring out the character of the protagonists and offer a contrast to their behaviour in peace prior to or following their behaviour in war. As Bromhead has demonstrated, what gives the film *Chariots of Fire* its power is the contrasting moral qualities of the athletes, Abrahams and Liddell. This may take some of the fun out of sport (is there much left?), but it makes good material for dramatic art.

English literature is full of descriptions of leisure of a less vigorous form than the athletic prowess described in Homer and Virgil, or, for that matter, in the Irish and Scandinavian sagas, and the lore of other peoples. Edward Larrissy proposes the thesis that not only did English writers (poets, novelists and dramatists) make refined pleasure and civilised living a subject matter to be written about – as did most writers on both sides of the Atlantic and from the Atlantic to the Urals – but they actually argued in defence of such a practice, from the eighteenth century onwards. It is in Blake; it dominates the writings of Pater; and it is to be found in the theory and practice of Wilde, Beerbohm, and the Bloomsbury Group.

It would be no exaggeration to say that the English treatment of leisure in its literature in the latter half of the Victorian era, and in the Edwardian era and beyond (wherever that era survived in attitudes to life and in imagination and dream) is unique. The Russians might claim Goncharov's *Oblomov* as belonging to the genre, but both the character and the whole tenor and thrust of the book are different. Oblomov, albeit born into the leisured aristocracy, is indolent, slothful and, finally, incapable of any activity that could be called pleasurable or leisure. Moreover, his story is the tragi-comic situation of the imaginative but ineffectual Russian aristocracy (or any effete and redundant aristocracy) in the modern world of practical entrepreneurs. Oblomov belongs to the world of the Ranevskis (*The Cherry Orchard*) or of Lermontov's hero (*A Hero of Our Times*) rather than to the world of Lord Emsworth, much less that of the Hon. Freddie Threepwood.

The essence of this genre is that the main, if not the entire, subject matter of the work is leisure activity. Jerome K. Jerome's *Three Men in a Boat* fits firmly into the genre, but, though Jerome went on to write *Three Men on the Bummel* ten years later (1900) and founded the humorous periodical *The Idler* (to which Mark Twain contributed), he was an incidental practitioner of the genre compared with Sir Pelham Grenville Wodehouse.

As Stephen Ickringill says in his paper, leisure is the sole topic of Wodehouse's output. None of his principal characters have to earn a living. They live off inherited wealth or allowances or what they can borrow or acquire through ingenuity. They engage in the pursuits of the leisured – entertaining and being entertained, frequenting their clubs, enjoying themselves in their ample domains. Very few characters, with the exception of the efficient Baxter and some of the females of the species, do serious work. Even the butlers, Jeeves and Beech, are drawn into this leisurely existence, retiring to their pantries or clubs when their not-too-arduous duties have been fulfilled with consummate ease and efficiency. And yet the lives of these characters are not beds of roses. They may not sit as magistrates or in the House of Peers or be in any way useful to society, and yet it might have been better for them if they were. Relieved of the worries of trying to make a living, they are beset with the problems of day-to-day life. Aunts, nephews, nieces, close friends, casual acquaintances continually make trouble for them. It may not be the trouble that befalls a protagonist in a Greek tragedy, but it is trouble enough.

Sean O'Casey was disgusted with the adulation lavished on Wodehouse by Belloc, Orwell and others. He could not see how anyone could take him seriously. (I have heard the same said by an eminent French critic of O'Casey.) He writes comedies. They have happy endings. In life there are few happy endings. He deals with the leisured classes and ignores the problems of the poor, the homeless, the unemployed. True. Ickringill concedes this, but says that Wodehouse was aware of it, and concentrated on the problems of the leisured classes. They have problems too, as do all of humankind. Of all people O'Casey should be the last to criticise Wodehouse, being the man who made fun of the Dublin working class to which he himself belonged.

However, O'Casey may have a point. Not even the staunchest admirers of Wodehouse could attribute great social criticism to his work (if that is to be taken as a criterion of depth and greatness). Nor would one have thought that Kenneth Grahame was a prime candidate for that honour. However, George Hyde, in an ingenious analysis of *The Wind in the Willows*, shows how much psychological and socio-historical significance there is in it. It is undoubtedly about leisure – life on the river ('messing about in boats') in an idyllic Edwardian pre-war eternal summer (not unlike Wodehouse's), with motoring cars for pleasure and an animal Blandings, Toad Hall. But, as Hyde demonstrates, there are, behind these blissful or seemingly childish and certainly amusing episodes, rather serious moral implications. The moral character of these animals (humanised) exposes human moral defects (and virtues). Mole and Rat are not all that good, and Toad, the villain of the piece, is more foolish and vain than wicked.

Attributing moral, psychological or even sociological characteristics to animals is not confined to the English or to modern literature. Aesop did it, and so did many others. What is peculiar to the English, if Hyde is to be believed (and there is every reason that he should be), is that, under the appearance of telling a bed-time story, they were putting across moral ideas. There is nothing particularly new in this. What is new is that, unlike the heroic tales of Homer and Virgil, theirs are about animals or toys. (Pooh bear was not mentioned.)

But for all that, Wodehouse and Grahame cannot be regarded as more than minor writers. Certainly not in the same league as Goncharov. Lewis Carroll, who is mentioned, was more serious a writer because of the various layers of meaning he wove into his stories. But in the Alice books leisure is rather the setting than the subject: they are not so much about leisure or the leisured class as about what can happen as leisure activities in an extraordinary world – mad hatter's tea parties, croquet played with flamingoes, living chess pieces and suchlike. While leisure as depicted in literature, whether vigorous and even violent, in Homer and Virgil, or tranquil, dreamy or inconsequential, in Wodehouse and Grahame, as a subject in its own right and for its own sake does not seem to be the stuff of great literature, yet in the texture of an epic, play, story or novel it can have great weight and significance. In the visual arts, however, matters are somewhat different.

As I try to show in my paper on leisure in Western art, painters, in their (possibly unconscious) effort to emancipate their art from the demands of religion, politics and social concern, turned to the depiction of leisure. In so doing they were establishing the essential of painting itself as a leisure activity. Along with instrumental music and dance, which are quintessentially leisure activities, painting, unlike literature, has the potentiality to be a wholly leisure activity, that is, one indulged in for its own sake and for the pleasure it gives. Painting a landscape or a still life may not seem like a leisure activity, nor the subject matter to be a leisure activity; but a moment's reflection shows that they are. First, the very looking at a landscape *as a landscape* and not as fields to be ploughed or pastures to be grazed or mountains to be crossed is a leisure activity, whether one strolls through it or not. And as for flowers and fruit or even game, they are for gracious living. Secondly, in painting such subjects the artist can make free use of his skill and imagination.

Moreover, even if humans are introduced into these pictures – bathing, boating, at the theatre, sitting in a garden, eating in a café or al fresco – they too can be treated as no more than visual objects (like studio nudes), objects on which to hang colour, and to arrange in a certain order. They need carry no message, religious, moral, social or political, since the activities they depict do not have even a nominal relation to any of these values. And this is the difference between painting and literature in relation to leisure.

The depth of literature lies, as has been said, in both the weight of the subject matter and the weight of creative construction. In painting, creative construction can be all and the weight of the subject matter nil. Seurat's *Bathers at Asnières* represents no event (other than the supposed original grouping of the figures, which is doubtful), has no moral (other than: 'take your rest as you think fit' or some such) and is yet a picture of some degree of profundity. One can read out of it what one wills, but each figure in the landscape has his (there are no females present) own attitude to life. This is a picture of leisure if ever there was one – people in the water, one almost swimming, on the edge of the water, on the grass, sitting up, lying down, and yachts sailing in the distance against a backdrop of industrial pollution, and all in glorious sunshine.

The art of the twentieth century carried this a stage further when it became a playing with colours and shapes and space, conspicuously the free play of the imagination and understanding, as Kant described the aesthetic activity. Leisure subjects continued to be used – the café scene, dancing, the circus, etc. – but, with abstract and semi-abstract art (Mondrian, Klee, Schwitters, Kandinsky) art tended towards the condition of the free play of music or dancing. And literature did so also: the free play of words and images, as in Formalist poems and plays, successors to nonsense verse and the plays of Jarry, and forerunners of concrete poetry and the plays of Beckett.

From art for its own sake we turn to art in the service of education, and from leisure as an adjunct to art to leisure as an enemy of art and learning, though not of moral development. This is right, if we regard the relationship of leisure, art and literature from an English rather than a British (Welsh, Scottish or Irish) point of view. Just as the English literature and painting (though not much of it) reflected the leisured affluence of the English upper class between the 1870s and World War I, so the use to which classical literature was put in public schools during this period and the effect that use had on university education at Oxbridge are uniquely English. The other British, and the colonists and colonised of the British Empire, were infected by it, but it remained essentially English.

Thomas Arnold was responsible for this, and he pervades this volume as he pervaded English education for over a century. As Malcolm Tozer tells the story, Arnold set the tone with his Platonic-Christian ideal of a balanced education in which physical fitness and team spirit were to have a favourable moral influence on the young. But matters got out of hand (according to one's point of view) and the Spartans took over from the Athenians, as Tozer puts it. Arnold's, Thring's and Almond's reasonable insistence on the importance of games in a school curriculum led to a cult of sport to the detriment of scholarship. There was also a shift from the Plato of the *Republic* and the *Laws* to the Homer of heroic deeds. Besides games, following the disasters of the Boer War, there were officers' training corps and youths ready to perform deeds of Homeric valour. This dream floundered in the trenches and the mud of Flanders Field.

J. A. Mangan takes up the narrative as it unfolds in higher education in Oxford and Cambridge. They carried on where the public schools had left off, but with less reason. A lad was either formed in character and morals by the time he was of university age or he never would be. Yet, by the late nineteenth century, the public-school adulation of team games such as rowing (above all), rugby football and cricket took precedence over scholarship to the extent that to get a blue was vastly more desirable than to get a double first. Thus a full circle had been completed. The classics, Homer and Plato in particular, had generated athleticism, and athleticism in turn had led to the eclipse of the classics as a moral driving force. The achievements of Abrahams and Liddell at the Olympic Games in Paris in 1924 were, probably, the last flash of a setting sun that began its descent well before Passchendaele, and the film *Chariots of Fire* (which is a recurrent theme of the volume) reflects this admirably.

So what are we to say about leisure in art and literature?

Many things.

First we could say that the view of leisure in this volume is too English. That in itself might not be a bad thing. Leisure is as universal in art, as we have seen, as it is in literature. But in literature its treatment takes on a more local flavour. Popular revelry is much the same in Brueghel, Velazquez, Hals and Hogarth. A genteel party in the garden is much the same if painted by Renoir, Seurat, Lavery, Osborne or one of the Italian Impressionists. Leisure as described in literature more closely reflects the temperament and culture that produces it. It is hard to imagine the goings-on in Blandings Castle or Toad Hall or the Drones Club having a counterpart in a French château, German schloss or Italian palazzo. And as for the Drones, they have a few near counterparts abroad, but this is because their founders were English or wished to imitate the English model.

Why, then, not call the book *Leisure in English Art, Literature and Education*? This would approximate to what the book is about but not to what the book aims to do, which is to take a wider view of leisure as depicted in art and literature. This Winnifrith and I have attempted. It so happens that what Winnifrith has to say about games in Homer and Virgil has direct references of diverse kinds to English public school and university education. That might, and should, be regarded as accidental. It was certainly not planned when we set out on this particular road of research. What has emerged, therefore, in response to our invitations to collaborate on this topic is the peculiar Englishness of the English depictions of leisure, while we do not entirely ignore the world outside.

What have been ignored, or barely mentioned, are such leisure activities as music and dancing. These, it will be said, are leisure activities *par excellence*, indulged in by everyone from peasant to duke. They would make an interesting topic for a volume in their own right. And, indeed, such books exist. But for our purposes this would be to make the topic too specialised. At most we could have afforded a paper on each; say, on children's games portrayed in music (Saint-Saëns, Debussy, Britten, Stravinsky) or the pastoral in ballet, e.g. *Prélude à l'après-midi d'un faune*, as choreographed by Diaghilev, from a score by Debussy, based on a poem by Mallarmé and first danced by Nijinsky. Here we have the portrayal of leisure *by* music and dance, and that is what is needed for this volume. More might have been said of music and dance as portrayed in literature and painting. But they have at least been mentioned. Watteau and Degas were fascinated by dance and celebrated it in paint. But it would not be quite so easy to celebrate it in literature unless one was portraying a balletomane or someone besotted by music, such as the maharajah so wonderfully depicted in Ray's film *The Music Room*. (It is a rare musician or dancer who regards his or her life as one of leisure.)

Finally, it might be said that the volume is rather too heavily weighted towards the leisure activities of the upper classes and that there has not been sufficient social comment. This, up to a point, is a valid criticism. We could have published a paper from another volume on, say, Sickert's music-hall pictures. And the fact that our subject was not the sociology of leisure or even the sociology of the depiction of leisure in art and literature is no excuse for not making a passing reference to it. We do, in fact, make some passing references – Hyde is socially conscious in his treatment of Toad in relation to the other animals and draws attention to the fact that, when Grahame was writing, the life they led was enjoyed by very few. And this is the truth of the matter. In the Middle Ages it was the nobility and upper clergy who enjoyed leisure, except at festival time, weddings and such rare occasions. After the industrial revolution and urbanisation matters got worse: for most people the only recreation was the pub and the Saturday football match or the occasional boxing match. All this has been recorded in art and literature. But, with the possible exception of Jack B. Yeats, no artists or writers have celebrated it or made it the main subject of their art. It is usually incidental: local colour. So, to make leisure the quintessential subject of art and literature, the writer or artist must take the activities of the so-called leisured classes (to which most of us, in varying degrees of elegance, now belong) as his subject.

What we have tried to show in this book is that the arts and literature are essentially leisure activities. This is most manifest when their subject matter is leisure. This, however, does not in any way mean that the depiction of leisure may not be serious. Nor does it mean that the depiction and portrayal of the most serious subjects – religious, moral, historical, political, and so forth – is not a leisure activity (however physically and mentally arduous). It is play, albeit serious play. To be successful as art or literature, it must be, as Kant says, the *free play* of the imagination and the understanding. In this it differs from designers' drawings or government reports (though these may have some imaginative content even if they offer little to the understanding). But ultimately most of the more serious mental activities are both leisure activities and serious – mathematics, science, even philosophy itself are all scholastic activities. However, it would be disingenuous to suggest that the depiction of these activities in art and literature, and the use of these depictions in education, were among the most serious of human activities. There are subjects such as warfare, starvation, exploitation, the struggle to survive, terrorism and suchlike unpleasant and undesirable human activities that are far more serious in human life. Nevertheless, the leisure activities of art and literature do not ignore them. They portray and reflect on them and, thus, help us to come to terms with them; but when they portray leisure itself they show what ought to be, in what the joyous fulfilment of the potential of human life consists.

1

Funeral Games in Homer and Virgil

Tom Winnifrith

In spite of much recent critical commentary on Virgil and Homer there has not been a great deal of attention paid to the funeral games in book 23 of the *Iliad* and book 5 of the *Aeneid*.[1] The admirable critical commentaries of Willcock and Williams, to whom I owe an obvious debt, are full of useful information, but both tend to dismiss the games as intervals of light relief inserted to give the participants and the reader an escape from the tension and drama in the preceding and succeeding books.[2] Explorations of the different philosophies of the two epic poets have somehow neglected the games as admirable opportunities for each poet to state his contrasting philosophy. In spite of the fact that classics and cricket used to be, and in some old-fashioned quarters still are, regarded as two cornerstones of English education, students of leisure have neglected two of the earliest and greatest descriptions of a sporting event as important contributions to the study of sporting morality.

The games are funeral games in honour of Patroklos and Anchises; celebrating a funeral in this way is something which modern readers find hard to understand, but the awareness of the funeral adds solemnity and importance to the epic accounts. Book 22 of the *Iliad*, telling of the death of Hektor at the hands of Achilles, and book 24, recounting how Achilles gives Hektor's body back to Priam, clearly involve high drama and deep significance, as do books 4 and 6 of the *Aeneid*, but the surrounding books must add interest to the games that bridge the gap. Book 22 shows Achilles and life so full of savagery that we need the games to provide the link with book 24 when Achilles and life are full of sorrow. Likewise the games in book 5 may help to connect the weary wanderer of the first part of the *Aeneid* with the wary warrior of the second part, whose mission, so clearly stated in book 6, is some-

14

what obscurely bungled in book 4. Similarly, students of the philosophy of sport should not be discouraged by the slightly odd sporting events in Homer and Virgil, because both poets, in a timeless fashion, express definite and almost definitive attitudes to questions of sport.

Homer's games have eight events. Doubts have been cast upon the short and not very illuminating analyses of the fight in armour, the discus and the archery, seen as late additions to a canon of five events. These events are described twice during the chariot race as constituting a pentathlon of the chariot race, the boxing, wrestling, footrace and javelin, which Achilles mentions to Nestor and about which Nestor reminisces with garrulous but innocent boastfulness. Virgil has a boat race, clearly adapted from Homer's chariot race, both races involving turning round a mark, changes of lead and the taking of risks. Certain elements of the chariot race, including the many contestants and the dispute about the results, have been transferred to Virgil's foot race which does have as its central feature, as in Homer, a fall by one of the runners. Both Homer and Virgil have boxing matches with similar contestants, but a very different outcome. Virgil's archery contest is an extension of Homer's competition. The miraculous conclusion, whereby the arrow of Acestes bursts into flame, is something that could never have happened in Homer, although the gods do intervene in both poems. There is probably a historical allusion here to the comet which appeared in 44 BC, the year in which Julius Caesar was assassinated and Octavian instituted games in his honour. Certainly the *lusus Troiae*, in which Ascanius and other Trojan youths performed military manoeuvres, refers to a ceremony encouraged by both Caesar and Augustus.[3]

These particular historical allusions may blind us to the universal quality of Homer's and Virgil's sporting narrative. In the *Iliad* Epeios claims the prize for the boxing before there is any contest. His boasting puts off other competitors until Euryalos is persuaded to enter the ring. In nineteenth-century school stories it is the braggarts who lose and the reluctant underdogs who win unexpected but deserved triumphs, but in Homer and in real life, as Muhammed Ali so often proved, the man who says that he is the greatest very often is the greatest. Epeios wins by a knockout, chivalrously helping his opponent away from the fight. Epeios has, as Muhammed Ali had, brains as well as brawn because, though he makes a fool of himself in the discus, and says he is not a particularly good warrior, he was the man who devised the wooden horse. Even his boasting is not all that offensive, much less so than that of Dares, a very much less pleasant character, his arrogant counterpart in Virgil, who struts about, claiming that nobody can beat him, but in fact is knocked out. In Virgil the nineteenth-century public school ethos is in control, but the atmosphere is much more savage. This is partly because in Homer, as in modern boxing matches, the gloves worn are there to protect the hands, whereas in Virgil and in Roman boxing matches the *caestus* lined with metal could maim and kill an opponent. This makes the contest a much more bloodthirsty one, even though the victor, Entellus, shows restraint in victory, is reluctant to fight, and appears at first sight about to lose. We are of course reminded of this contrast between Dares and Entellus when we compare Turnus's behaviour in battle with that of Aeneas, whereas in Homer Achilles, like Epeios, boasts that nobody is a match for him, and nobody is. There is not in Homer the belief that behaving well somehow wins matches and battles.

In Virgil's boat race some behave and do well, namely Cloanthus, the winner, and Mnestheus, whom he beats by a canvas; whereas Gyas, who throws his helmsman overboard, and Sergestus, who takes unnecessary risks, are punished for their conduct. This bad conduct is something more complicated than Dares's boastfulness, although still easily recognisable to those who see sport as a moral educator. Gyas' treatment of his helmsman, Menoetes, shows him a poor leader of men, whereas Mnestheus's success comes after a rousing speech in which he appeals to his men's team spirit. Gyas urges Menoetes to take risks by cutting corners. This is unwise because Sergestus badly damages his boat by steering too close to the rocks. It may be asked what is wrong with taking risks, but the *Aeneid* is full of warnings against those who, like Turnus and Nisus and Euryalus, are led by too great a desire for personal glory into acts of rashness. One can hear through Virgil's narrative the pompous voices of the schoolmasters of one's youth not only urging the virtues of team spirit but also warning against letting the side down by some rash stroke or kick or individual run or dribble. It is just possible that Virgil may have a particular grudge against Sergestus. He stresses unnecessarily that from him the *gens* Sergia was derived. The most notorious member of this *gens* was Lucius Sergius Catilina, a man conspicuous for taking rash short cuts in his search for glory.[4]

It is all very different in Homer. With teams of horses rather than men there can be less emphasis on team spirit. Antilochos does give a rousing speech to his horses, saying, like Mnestheus, that it will be disgraceful to fare badly, but, unlike Mnestheus, threatening his team with death if they do not try a little harder. There is intervention by the gods, but in a very arbitrary fashion as first Diomedes then Eumelos loses his whip at the whim of Apollo and Athene. This is very different from the solemn way in which Cloanthus's pious prayer is uttered and rewarded. Piety is of course a moral virtue, if not *the* moral virtue, in the *Aeneid*; *Chariots of Fire* excepted, it has not had much of a run in modern sport, although in games where chance plays as much a part as skill there is still the irrational feeling that virtue can affect good fortune in the same way that practice can enhance skill. Even Antilochos, a cheerful and unsolemn participant, says that Eumelos should have prayed to the gods, although Antilochos is perhaps over-anxious for his own prize which Achilles is tempted to give to Eumelos as a consolation for his bad luck.[5]

Antilochos gains the second prize because Achilles finds a special reward for Eumelos, but he has to ward off another challenge for this prize from Menelaos, who claims that he has been cheated out of it by some reckless driving on the part of his younger rival. Here is another obvious contrast between Homer and Virgil. Sergestus and Gyas fail because they take risks or are too keen to take risks, whereas Antilochos owes his success to his youthful daring. His father Nestor, like a wiser Polonius, gives him some lengthy but shrewd advice on just how close to the turning post he can go, although it is in fact on the return run, in a narrower part of the course, that Antilochos takes his calculated risk. After a few angry words at the beginning of the dispute Menelaos and Antilochos then try and outdo each other in gentlemanly behaviour, each in turn offering to give his prize to the other. Bad behaviour is much more prominent among the spectators, like Idomeneus and the lesser Aias, who swap insults and inaccurate information in a fashion all too familiar to the detached observer of a modern sporting occasion. As in Virgil's boat race, and indeed in *Alice in Wonderland*, everybody gets prizes, although in Homer there is the added satisfaction of an extra prize for Nestor who, as coach and commentator, has the irritating charm of Jack Charlton and John Arlott rolled into one.

Homer's chariot race occupies what may seem a disproportionate length, taking nearly twice as long to describe as the other seven events added together. In Virgil, though the boat race is similarly the first and longest contest to be described, there is much less disparity, and we might be tempted to admire the artistic neatness of Virgil's arrangement and to deplore Homer's rough and ready scramble through the later events. In fact Homer's arrangement can be defended. Some sporting events are best described at length, others more briefly. John Arlott would be out of place at a football match, still more so at the Derby. By inserting the spectators, the memories of former matches, the quarrel about the results and the advice of the coach into one event Homer is able to show the relationship between the different facets of a sporting event.

Virgil, in order to make his pattern more compact, has occasionally switched episodes or motifs from one Homeric event to another in his scheme where two shorter events follow the longer boat race and boxing match. Thus Odysseus's prayer in the foot race is presumably the model for Cloanthus's successful prayer in the boat race, whereas Virgil's foot race has the suspicion of foul play and subsequent quarrel which originated in Antilochos's conduct in the chariot race. In spite of annual warnings delivered to the coxes by the umpire at the beginning of the Oxford and Cambridge boat race, cheating is fairly difficult in rowing, and accusations of foul play in sailing are largely confined to the building of the boat. So, in Virgil's boat race, where oars and sails are both needed, it would have been difficult to introduce that particular brand of bad sportsmanship. In running, however, as Mary Decker and Peter Elliot have sadly proved, there is bumping and boring, and therefore a practical as well as an artistic reason why Virgil has included the dispute in the foot race. In Homer's foot race there is a fall, but no real dispute. While Odysseus and Aias are fighting it out for first place Odysseus prays to Athene for inspiration and Aias accidentally slips in some dung, but recovers to come second. The race must be quite a long one for this to happen and to enable Antilochos, well beaten by his elders, to come in third and make a graceful speech, disarming the bad-tempered Aias as he had previously disarmed Menelaos. Aias had shown his bad temper as a spectator in the chariot race. In coming second and being beaten by Odysseus he reminds us of his namesake, Telamonian Aias, who finished second in three events; this Aias is clearly, though a gallant second-row forward, not one of nature's winners, in sport or in life.[6] Homer has many characters who take part in many events, and with Antilochos and Aias he is able to draw conclusions through this versatility; with fewer events and fewer well known competitors Virgil is less able to do this, and we do not draw many lessons from the fact that Mnestheus comes second in the boat race and third in the archery.[7]

On the other hand Virgil does want to make more of his much more complicated foot race. It appears to be a much shorter course. This is clear both from images of speed and from the fact that on this occasion the two contestants have no time to recover. Nisus slips in the gore resulting from the sacrifice of some animals. Dung is sufficient for Homer and the more homely *Georgics*, but less suitable for Virgil's more elevated epic. And yet, what happens in the foot race is far from elevated. Nisus drags the second runner Salius with him, thus allowing his beloved friend Euryalus to come in first, and the otherwise totally obscure Helymus and Diores, who have been fighting it out for fourth place, to make second and third position. But the result as announced is unpopular. Salius appeals, saying that he deserves the first prize, Euryalus says nothing, winning favour by his modest silence and good looks, while Diores, seeing that he may be robbed of the bronze medal, makes angry protests. There is a faint whiff of Sports Day at Llanabba Castle in Evelyn Waugh's *Decline and Fall* as Aeneas, smiling with the false geniality of a preparatory school headmaster in a tight spot, manages to dig up a prize for Salius and then for Nisus who claims that he too has been robbed. Nisus's claim seems hardly to be justified. Any properly conducted Stewards' Enquiry would have banned him from the course for at least a year, and Aeneas surely errs in not condemning him. Unlike Achilles, who has a prize for every competitor, and even one in reserve for Nestor, Aeneas has no reward for people like Patron and Panopes who join the race but never get a mention in it, or the many besides who do not even get a mention in Wisden and who leave the field as unsatisfied as the reader.[8]

Homer's games occur at the end of the *Iliad*, a long poem involving a long war. Heroes like Menelaos, Aias and Odysseus play a major part in the games, in the rest of the poem, and in the war, of which only a very small part is described in the *Iliad*. In the *Aeneid* there is less room for heroes apart from Aeneas, and, though the games might have served a useful purpose in introducing Trojans who were going to fight as hard in war as on the playing field like some Newbolt hero, Virgil eschews this opportunity. This eschewal is

clearly deliberate in an epic which both aims to subordinate the
individual in the interests of the common good and looks to
long-term universal peace rather than a short-term nationalistic
war. Of the major contestants in the foot race Nisus, Euryalus and
Diores are all Trojans, Salius is a Greek who presumably joined
Aeneas at Buthrotum, and Helymus is a Sicilian. Nationalist fervour may add a little edge to the fervour of the contestants,
although Virgil, in making Entellus and Acestes, both Sicilians,
win the boxing and the archery, is clearly not eager, here or
anywhere else in the *Aeneid*, to pursue a narrow nationalist line.

Nisus, Euryalus and Diores all die in the latter part of the *Aeneid*.
Diores is killed by Turnus in book 12, and Nisus and Euryalus die
in book 9 as a result of the night raid in Aeneas's absence. This raid
is modelled on the more successful adventure of Odysseus and
Diomedes in book 10 of the *Iliad*. Nisus and Euryalus are led astray
from their original intention to summon help for the beleaguered
Trojans by what might seem to be a crude combination of Homeric
virtues and Virgilian vices, namely bloodlust, love of glory and a
desire for booty both as a mark of this glory and as a good in itself.
Praise and money, the two corrupters of mankind according to Dr
Johnson, clearly enter into Nisus's mind even before he has volunteered to try and reach Aeneas. In a significant passage he asks
himself whether it is a god or his own ambition which inspires
him. This may hark back to Odysseus's prayer to Athene in the
foot race of book 23. Obviously the gods cannot be invoked to
support the dirty tricks in book 5, and Nisus has got the gods
wrong in book 9. Had he modelled himself on Cloanthus, to whom
Odysseus's prayer has been transferred in a more solemn form, all
might have been well in both books 5 and 9. As it is, in both books
Virgil's verdict on Nisus and Euryalus is curiously mixed. Euryalus's modesty, silence and beauty are emphasised but, unlike
Antilochos, he makes no effort to give his prize back.[9] In book 9 it
is Euryalus's love of shining prizes, in this case the gleaming
helmet of Messapus, which leads to the death of both Trojans.
Nisus's demand for a prize in book 5, wearily granted by Aeneas,
seems as grasping as his desire for glory in book 9, and yet Virgil,
while clearly condemning the Homeric love of glory, gives, as so
often, an ambiguous verdict on both Nisus and Euryalus. Like
Dido and Turnus, two other losers who sought to be winners,
Nisus and Euryalus are granted praise as well as blame.

The final verdict on the unlucky pair is 'fortunati ambo'.[10] This must call into question Virgil's and Aeneas's failure to condemn the unfortunate antics of book 5. Of course neither in book 5, nor in book 9, is Nisus entirely selfish. His love for Euryalus is as important as loyalty to his team, and Virgil can see the conflict. But Aeneas, torn by the same conflict in book 4, could have handled the dispute differently in book 5, and would have done so if he had progressed very far in his transition from hesitation to single-minded dutifulness. Unfortunately, in book 9, when he has made this transition, he is not present to restrain Nisus's ardour. Achilles, who has his own transition to make from being the bloodthirsty savage of book 22 to the great gentleman of book 24, is the model of tact that Aeneas is meant and sometimes claimed to be. He not only sorts out the disputes in the chariot race, but stops Diomedes and Aias murdering each other in the fight in armour, prevents the rivalry between Odysseus and Aias getting out of hand in the wrestling, and finally, in the javelin, awards the prize to Agamemnon without a contest. This is not just a pleasant gesture like allowing the Duke of Edinburgh to score runs in a match in which Test cricketers are playing. It is a reminder that the grim quarrel between Achilles and Agamemnon is over, and also, since the javelin is the last event, a reminder that the real world where Agamemnon is supreme is about to take over from the world of the games.

Virgil's last event of a competitive nature is the archery contest. Here he seeks to improve upon Homer's account of a similar contest by making it longer and adding a moral. In the *Iliad* there are two entrants aiming at a bird attached to a mast. Teukros hits the string, Meriones the bird, and there are prizes for both. Virgil has four contestants, of whom Hippocoon hits the mast, Mnestheus the string, Eurytion the bird, and Acestes wins because of the miraculous transformation of his arrow into a fiery comet. The four competitors remind us of the four entries in the boat race, especially as Mnestheus takes part in both events, and in both the first and the last contest there is supernatural intervention. Eurytion, like Mnestheus in the boat race, makes a supreme effort, appealing to the memory of his brother Pandarus as Mnestheus had appealed to his men, but the gods have Cloanthus and Acestes more in favour.

No doubt Virgil thought he had improved on Homer, although as a contest the archery event has roughly the same excitement as a televised darts match. The idea that piety is what counts in winning matches is, as we have shown, a misplaced one. Virgil has, however, another moral in store for us. In the previous three events there has been bad behaviour. Sergestus, Gyas, Dares and practically all the front runners in the foot race disgrace themselves in some way, and yet even Sergestus with his shattered boat and the unconscious Dares get prizes. In the archery all perform creditably, and Eurytion, faced with a moving target, instead of asking for an adjournment, performs outstandingly. And yet the one prize goes to Acestes. One could not have a better illustration of the hoary line of Newbolt that the game is worth more than the prize, a lesson reinforced by the fact that the next event, the *lusus Troiae*, has no prizes at all.

Throughout this analysis of Homer's and Virgil's games I have been awarding more points to Homer than to Virgil. Admirers of Virgil may feel that this is unfair, and that I have failed to bring out the later poet's skill and artistry in transforming Homer's rough and ready chronicle into definite moral and artistic patterns. In a way, comparing Homer with Virgil is like comparing *War and Peace* with *The Golden Bowl*, with the difference that though James disapproved of Tolstoy's loose baggy monsters he did not set out to rewrite them. Virgil's moral overtones may seem attractive to those brought up to believe that games are vehicles of moral instruction; and indeed clichés like team spirit, fair play, not letting the side down, rocking the boat, playing up and playing the game, seem to be behind Virgil's poetry, exciting and original though this poetry is. One is sometimes surprised on rereading Virgil not to find him echoing the singular and fatuous advice that I heard in my youth, to the effect that if one played with a straight bat at cricket one played with a straight bat in life. As I have argued elsewhere,[11] there is a confusion in the idea that sport can be, and should be, a moral educator, attractive though this idea is when so much of sport today is tarnished by commercialism and involves cheating and violence.

In the past hundred years we have seen games decline and fall from their original function as a relaxing and amusing leisure activity to being a deplorable opportunity for chauvinism, brawling and dishonesty. The centenary of the modern Olympic games in 1996 is a useful reminder of this change, although the original founders of the games in 1896 were filled with the moral idealism and high seriousness which we have been gently mocking when we see it in the work of Virgil. By taking games too seriously as moral educators the Virgilian idealists of the late nineteenth and early twentieth century did pave the way to games being exploited for less worthy causes. Curiously we can see the same pattern being repeated in epic poetry in the hundred years after Virgil. Virgil has taken away the innocence and good humour of Homer's games, but his lofty heroes are a great improvement on the games in Statius's *Thebaid* and Silius Italicus's *Punica*.[12]

Statius' games are held by the Argive army, later to be defeated. Virgil gives no hint that Nisus and Euryalus will repeat their behaviour in the context of war, but Statius gives several heavy-handed hints that the participants in the games have sterner struggles ahead of of them. Not that the games in Statius provide much in the way of light relief. The chariot race has all the fury of *Ben Hur* and is actually likened to a war. There are bad crashes which could have been fatal; rather tactlessly Statius says that it might have saved many lives if Polynices had been killed. In the foot race the leading runner Parthenopaeus has his hair pulled by Idas behind him, a piece of trickery which far exceeds that of Nisus, but which pleases some of the spectators. Adrastus, in charge of the games, orders a rerun with the two leading runners in lanes, and appropriately Parthenopaeus wins, but the episode leaves a nasty taste. There is then a long account of the discus, not, one would have thought, an event likely to point a moral or adorn a tale, although Statius does his best with the disappointing performance of Phlegyas, later to be repeated in the war. The boxing is far more savage than in Virgil, and far less satisfactory with the boastful and violent Capaneus, whose blasphemous death is here foreshadowed, chasing Alcidamas all over the ring but unable to finish him off because Alcidamas evades his blows. The match ends in a rather unsatisfactory draw with Adrastus intervening to prevent murder being committed. There is a result in the wrestling, with the strength and fury of Tydeus overcoming Argylleus, but the fight in armour is stopped on the grounds that real war is imminent, and the games end portentously with Adrastus shooting an arrow which mysteriously returns to him. This obviously augurs ill for Adrastus's army, and it is fairly easy to draw pointed comparisons between the feats and behaviour of the Argives in the games and their subsequent fates. Not surprisingly, since these fates are almost invariably unhappy, there is a gloomy atmosphere about Statius's games, the narration of which is marred by a desire to improve on Virgil with spectacular effects.

Silius's games are neither so spectacular nor so solemn. They are held in Spain to celebrate Scipio's success in wresting that province from Hannibal, and the victorious army shows none of the gloom of Statius's Argives. There are still crashes in the chariot race and hair–pulling in the foot race with no rebuke for either offence. The games end with Scipio throwing a spear which sprouts into a tree, a happy if silly reversal of the ill omen of Adrastus. The competitors do not play an important part in the war, and apart from the episode of the spear there is therefore no opportunity to draw parallels between games and battles. Silius is an epic poet without much inspiration, and we feel that his games are heavily derivative, but they can be used to trace not only the degeneration of epic into a collection of stock motifs, but also the dangers of taking games too seriously.

If behind Virgil and inspired by Virgil there are a lot of pompous schoolmasters talking about straight bats and playing the game, behind Statius and Silius Italicus there are cricketers who wear helmets and argue with the umpire. Baron de Coubertin was fired by Virgilian enthusiasm when he founded the modern Olympics, and some of the competitors who entered for that first Olympics had a Homeric *joie de vivre*. The modern Olympics, marred by politics, walkouts, assassinations and drug taking, and at the mercy of commercial interests and the squalor of capitalist society, represent the world of the gladiatorial arena pictured in Statius and Silius Italicus. This is a book about leisure and not about sport. Sport ceases to be a leisure activity when it is taken too seriously, and if Virgil's games hardly deserve a place in the history of leisure, the games in the *Thebaid* and the *Punica* certainly do not earn a place. I have only included them to show how a good idea of spending one's leisure can be corrupted. Homer had this good idea. Oddly, the occasion for his games is the most serious of any epic. Patroklos's funeral foreshadows, and may even be derived from, an account of Achilles's own funeral, and the universal shadow of death returns in book 24. The enjoyment of leisure in book 23 is Homer's answer to this shadow.

Notes

1. J. Griffin in *Life and Death in the Iliad* (Oxford, 1980) has three passing references to the games of book 23. C. W. McCleod, in his masterly

edition of *Iliad XXIV* (Cambridge, 1982), does mention the games, pp. 28–32, but chiefly with reference to Achilles's state of mind. M. Mueller, *The Iliad*, hardly considers the games at all. J. M. Redfield, *Nature and Culture in the Iliad* (Chicago, 1975) pp. 206–12 has some discussion of the games, but is chiefly concerned with prizes. Virgilian games are very briefly handled in K. Quinn, *Virgil's Aeneid, A Critical Description* (London, 1968). Brooks Otis has a long discussion of Virgil and Homer in *Virgil: A Study in Civilised Poetry* (Oxford, 1963), pp. 41–61 but chiefly, following R. Heinze, *Vergil's Epische Technik* (Leipzig, 1901), this discussion is mainly concerned with style. He tends to favour Virgil over Homer. More recent commentary has shied away from the games. There is, for instance, nothing in one of the best comparisons of Homer with Virgil, K. Gransden, *Virgil's Iliad* (Cambridge, 1989), concentrating as it does on the last six books of the *Aeneid*, and the short book on *Virgil* by J. Griffin (Oxford, 1986) just says twice that funeral games are held in book 5. There is a good chapter on the games in F. Cairns, *Virgil's Augustan Epic* (Cambridge, 1989) pp. 215–48, but very little in R. O. A. M. Lyne, *Further Voices in Vergil's Aeneid* (Oxford, 1986) or S. J. Harrison (ed.), *Oxford Readings in Vergil's Aeneid* (Oxford, 1990) or I. McCauslon and P. Walcot (eds), *Virgil* (Oxford, 1990). There is not much interest in the games as games in any of these writers. I have ignored for the purposes of this discussion the brief but pleasant account of the Phaeacian games in the *Odyssey*.

2. M. M. Willcock, *Iliad XII–XXIV* (London, or, for non-Greek readers, *A Companion to the Iliad* (Chicago, 1976), R. D. Williams *Aeneid V* (Oxford, 1962) or, more briefly, *Aeneid I–VI* (London, 1972).

3. Williams, *Aeneid I–VI*, pp. 432–3, although he has some doubts about the comet of 44 BC.

4. Williams, *Aeneid I–VI*, p. 406 mentions Catiline, but does not draw parallels between Sergestus's tactics and Catiline risking revolution rather than steering through constitutional waters.

5. In spite of Eric Liddell, a few sporting clergymen and the Irish team visiting the Pope during the World Cup, prayer and sport do not mix very well. A monotheistic religion cannot really cope with one God receiving prayers from two sides, as the Pope in Italy realised. Virgil is more monotheistic than Homer, where the gods' wilful and careless behaviour is admirably suited to the element of chance in any sporting occasion.

6. In a way, though the mighty Telamonian Aias seems not nimble enough to be a runner, particularly over a long distance, it would have made sense for him, rather than his lesser namesake, to slip in the dung and come second in view of the tragic outcome of his rivalry with Odysseus, in which slaughtered cattle also play a part.

7. Virgil has fewer constraints since, he is not limited by any oral tradition, and fewer major characters, since Trojans, apart from Aeneas, are not particularly prominent either before or after the games.

8. *Aeneid V*, 106. 'Multi praeterea quos fama obscura recondit'. The many besides, whose name history does not recall, seem to serve little

purpose and seem an aberration in view of the small entry in the other contests.

9. *Aeneid V*, 343–4. Words like 'favor' (popularity), 'lacrimae decorae' (modest tears) and the suggestion that his beauty helps his cause, while tactfully reinforcing the strong homosexual bond between Nisus and Euryalus, do not really excuse either party.

10. *Aeneid IX*, 446. Virgil goes on to express the hope that 'the fortunate pair' will gain eternal fame.

11. T. J. Winnifrith, 'Playing the Game' in T. J. Winnifrith and D. C. Barrett (eds), *The Philosophy of Leisure* (London, 1989) pp. 149–59.

12. Statius *Thebaid VI*, 234–946, Silius Italicus, *Punica XVI*, 277–591.

2
Leisure and Civilisation in English Literature

Edward Larrissy

Many have described the effects of the decline of patronage on writers' sense of their relationship with the public.[1] With the old system of patronage authors had a sense of belonging, even though they might be subject to the whims of their benefactor or of a relatively small group of subscribers. The market type of relationship which ensued was characterised by an unpredictability which was bound to be more inscrutable. Such a position need not entail a more acute sense of the effects of division of labour on society in general. But the writer's loss of an intimate audience, a close public, did facilitate a sense of the alienation inherent in the system as a whole. Yet these were not the terms in which writers tended to discuss the matter. Poets in particular, but not only poets, saw the origins of alienation in the gradual compartmentalisation and division of the various human capacities, leading up to the emergent industrial civilisation; original unalienated humanity, they felt, had expressed itself in poetic figures on all topics, and had accorded pride of place to professional poets, who were the repositories of the religious, legal, royal, historical and magical lore of the tribe, and were also regarded as prophets: the acknowledged legislators of mankind. Descriptions of the division of humanity are often, at the same time, accounts of how poetry has declined in social importance and, indeed, in energy and aesthetic value, and has become the province of an isolated and specialised élite.

The Romantic poets could consult a long and various tradition of antiquarian research in support of such ideas. Thomas Blackwell, in his *Enquiry into the Life and Writings of Homer* (1735), notes that the first Greek writings, 'as Oracles, Laws, Spells, Prophecies, were in Verse; and yet they got the simple Name of . . . Words or Sayings'.[2] For 'there was as yet no *Separation* of *Wisdom*: The Philosopher and the Divine, the Legislator and the Poet, were all united

27

in the same Person. Such was Orpheus . . .'[3] Not only Ancient Greeks, but Ancient Celts and Hebrews might be cited in evidence. A book which is very explicit about the breadth of powers possessed by the ancient bard is John Brown's *Dissertation on the Rise, Union, and Power, the Progressions, Separations, and Corruptions, of Poetry and Music* (1763). The 'barbarous *Legislators or Bards'*, he says,'sing songs of a *legislative* Cast; [which] being drawn chiefly from the Fables or History of their own Country, would contain the essential Parts of their *religious, moral*, and *political* Systems'.[4] It is interesting to see how the first thinkers who approximate to the modern notion of a sociologist accept these accounts of the history of poetry. Adam Ferguson's *Essay on the History of Civil Society* (1767) does so. It was translated into German by Christoph Garve in 1768, and subsequently read by Herder, Schiller, Hegel and Marx. Ferguson describes the poet as 'the first to offer the fruits of his genius, and to lead in the career of those arts by which the mind is destined to exhibit the imaginations, and to express its passions'.[5] And he concludes:

> The early history of all nations is uniform in this particular. Priests, statesmen, and philosophers, in the first ages of Greece, delivered their instructions in poetry, and mixed with the dealers in music and heroic fable.[6]

Along with the separation of disciplines goes a movement towards reason, veracity and abstraction:

> Men become interested by what was real in past transactions. They build on this foundation the reflections and reasonings they apply to present affairs, and wish to receive information on the subject of different pursuits, and of projects in which they begin to be engaged. . . . Mere ingenuity, justness of sentiment, and correct representation, though conveyed in ordinary language, are understood to constitute literary merit, and by applying to reason more than to the imagination and passions, meet with a reception that is due to the instruction they bring.[7]

In these circumstances 'a system of learning' may arise.[8] This system of learning will itself be the province of a specialised élite, as that other luminary of the Scottish Enlightenment, Adam Smith, explained:

In opulent and commercial societies to think or reason comes to be like every other employment, a particular business, which is carried on by a very few people, who furnish the public with all the thought and reason possessed by the vast multitudes that labour.[9]

Although the Romantic poet may profess, as did Wordsworth, distrust or contempt of the new reading 'Public', he may still feel tenderness towards 'the People',[10] and indignation at the lot of the masses employed in the machines of the new society, deprived of time and opportunity for reflection or for any but the crudest of aesthetic pleasures. Schiller had read Adam Ferguson, but although he was in broad agreement about the development of society, he was far more concerned in a moral sense:

Eternally tied to a single fragment of the whole, man himself develops into nothing but a fragment. Everlastingly in his ear is the monstrous sound of the wheel which he operates. He never develops the harmony of his being, and instead of stamping the imprint of humanity upon nature he becomes no more than the imprint of his occupation and his specialized knowledge.[11]

The opposite of this state is the ideal human wholeness exemplified for the Germans in the Greek *polis*, and justified in Goethe's famous assertions in *Dichtung und Wahrheit*: 'All that a man undertakes whether it be by deed or word must spring from the totality of his unified powers. Everything isolated is harmful.'[12] Such was the background to the analyses of alienation proffered by Hegel and Marx. The primitivist accounts of the development of poetry which form such an important part of that background may help to explain why attempts to define the unified, unfallen mode of consciousness sometimes take on an almost mystical colouring. Even Kant's idea of the free play of consciousness is probably indebted to such accounts.

Of all the English poets it is Blake who offers the most detailed and pondered reflections on the effects of the new industrial society both on the new proletariat and on the artist. Employed for the whole of his life as a commercial engraver of designs, usually by others, he felt a peculiarly intimate horror at the whole system:

Then left the sons of Urizen the plow & harrow, the loom,

> The hammer & the chisel & the rule & compasses.
> They forg'd the sword, the chariot of war, the battle ax,
> The trumpet fitted to the battle & the flute of summer,
> And all the arts of life they chang'd into the arts of death.
> The hour glass contemn'd because its simple workmanship
> Was as the workmanship of the plowman, & the water wheel
> That raises water into Cisterns, broken & burn'd in fire
> Because its workmanship was like the workmanship of the
>   shepherd,
> And in their stead intricate wheels invented, Wheel without
>   wheel,
> To perplex youth in their outgoings & to bind to labours
> Of day & night the myriads of Eternity, that they might file
> And polish brass & iron hour after hour, laborious
>   workmanship,
> Kept ignorant of the use that they might spend the days of
>   wisdom
> In sorrowful drudgery to obtain a scanty pittance of bread,
> In ignorance to view a small portion & think that All,
> And call it demonstration, blind to all the simple rules of
>   life.[13]

He allegorised the part of himself that laboured in isolation from the totality of his own powers as 'the Spectre'. As for 'Commerce', it is 'so far from being beneficial to Arts, or to Empires, that it is destructive of both'.[14] Behind this remark lurks the unstated notion that 'Commerce' is directed towards utilitarian ends and will not recognise a need to subsidise the artist. He wished for himself that he had been without the necessity of working:

> Some People & not a few Artists have asserted that the Painter of this Picture would not have done so well if he had been properly Encourag'd. Let those who think so, reflect on the State of Nations under Poverty & their incapability of Art; tho' Art is Above Either, the Argument is better for Affluence than Poverty; & tho' he would not have been a greater Artist, yet he would have produc'd Greater works of Art in proportion to his means.[15]

Poverty and the need to work for a living come down to a lack of time to pursue artistic endeavours, and even to a lack of the sort of time that might encourage the free play of the imagination. It is revealing to look at Blake's remarks about the 'Moment' of imagination in this light:

> There is a Moment in each Day that Satan cannot find
> Nor can his Watch Fiends find it; but the Industrious find
> This Moment & it multiply, & when it once is found
> It renovates every Moment of the Day if rightly placed.[16]

This is not merely a characteristically Romantic description of two sorts of time: the ambiguous 'Watch Fiends' can be seen as foremen, binding the artist to labours that can be measured by the clock.

The nineteenth century resounds with desperation at the absence of time for leisured feeding of the imagination and intellect. The note is memorably struck in the first lines of Wordsworth's sonnet:

> The world is too much with us; late and soon
> Getting and spending, we lay waste our powers:
> Little we see in nature that is ours;
> We have given our hearts away, a sordid boon!

('The World is Too Much With Us')

The emphasis, however, is different from Blake's. Where Blake, true to his craftsman's mentality, wants time for the timeless world of a different kind of work, Wordsworth, equally characteristically, wants time for an unhurried relationship with Nature, time to close up those barren leaves and wander without any 'useful' purpose, in the conviction that this is really one of the most useful things one can do. Wordsworth's poem finds a direct and lengthy echo in Matthew Arnold's 'Scholar Gypsy', the hero of which (no time-keeper) is apostrophised thus:

> O born in days when wits were fresh and clear,
> And life ran gaily as the sparkling Thames;
> Before this strange disease of modern life,
> With its sick hurry, its divided aims.

In his leisurely way, because free to ponder, free to follow his own hunch in the matter of learning, free to drop his books and draw inspiration from Nature, the Scholar Gypsy is undivided humanity: 'Thou hadst *one* aim, *one* business, *one* desire.' A modern person, however, 'half lives a hundred different lives'. The leisure Arnold desiderates is a space for the 'free play of thought' (echoes of Kant), for the disinterested spirit of enquiry, and for that spirit fed by a harmony of the human faculties, by 'harmonious perfection'.[17] He admits the necessity of industrial expansion, but sees it as a temporary stage, after which humanity's material needs will be met by machinery. He adverts to Gladstone's defence of capitalism, that it is necessary 'in order to lay broad foundations of material well-being for the society of the future'; but insists that as things stand 'the passing generations of Industrialists . . . are sacrificed to it'.[18] For history has imposed on them the necessity of living with stunted and divided powers, often unconscious that theirs is fools' gold, not least, perhaps, because the unswerving pursuit of gold has turned them into fools.

But such measured acceptance of necessity is not for all. The obvious alternative is, with Tennyson, to utter a plague on Locksley Hall: 'Cursed be the sickly forms that err from honest Nature's rule!/Cursed be the gold that gilds the straiten'd forehead of the fool!' ('Locksley Hall'). The cultivated but disturbed young narrator of this poem, jilted in favour of one who, we infer, enjoys the profits of industrialism, is tempted to escape to an oriental island:

> There methinks would be enjoyment more than in this march
> of mind
> In the steamship, in the railway, in the thoughts that shake
> mankind
>
> There the passions cramp'd no longer shall have scope and
> breathing space;
> I will take some savage woman, she shall rear my dusky race.

For poet, as for narrator, it is a temporary temptation: Tennyson comes to feel, as Alan Sinfield points out, that poet and capitalist are part of the same movement.[19] But others are not to be won over. There is a vital and subversive current which descends in a direct line from Keats through Brownig, the Pre-Raphaelites, and the Decadents, down to Bloomsbury and contemporary Bohemia. Although it conceives of leisure as a prerequisite of civilised, which is to say cultivated, existence, it does so in terms of the higher hedonism.

When Oscar Wilde asserts that 'Work is the curse of the drinking classes' he is not suggesting that the leisured classes should be earnest (at least, not according to the 'straight' definition). Rather he is alluding to an aristocratic manner of life in which the creation of art is the natural flowering of an existence in which the pleasures of conversation, love, friendship and art are the normal round and the proper goal. When Wilde visited Rome he kissed the Pope's hand. But the same evening, in the Protestant cemetery, he prostrated himself on Keats's grave.[20] In doing so he expressed a preference.

Keats asks for 'a life of sensations rather than thoughts'. He wishes to be freed from anxious ratiocination; but also from all touch of that, in what he calls 'real things', which might lead to thoughts directed to the world's approved ends. In this spirit he offers a partial cure for Melancholy:

> Then glut thy sorrow on a morning rose,
>   Or on the rainbow of the salt sand-wave,
>   Or on the wealth of globed peonies;
> Or if thy mistress some rich anger shows,
>   Emprison her soft hand, and let her rave,
>   And feed deep, deep upon her peerless eyes.

> (Ode on Melancholy)

This is highly 'aesthetic', indeed precious. It implies a life where enjoyment free of all taint of use is the true end. This is made especially clear by the way in which the mistress's message is ignored in favour of its fair manifestation. Such is the contemplative abstraction of Beauty from life that Keats offers as Truth. He reminds us that the moments in which such intensity is possible are transitory: 'She dwells with Beauty – Beauty that must die.' But the life into which such moments may enter cannot be bound by clock time, although this point is not made explicit in his work.

Not so with Browning. When his narrator's mind 'strays', in 'Two in the Campagna', physically and mentally through the land with his sweetheart on a May morning, Browning is flaunting not just the absent-minded, open-minded attitude, but the leisure that enables it. Into this attitude one of his eternal moments may enter: 'the good minute', as it is there described, in which he feels almost at one with his beloved. But the moment is transitory, though his very open-mindedness, his unwillingness to hold on to the moment, is the guarantee that such minutes will come again:

> Just when I seemed about to learn!
> Where is the thread now? Off again!
> The old trick! Only I discern –
> Infinite passion and the pain
> Of finite hearts that yearn.

In 'Up at a Villa – Down in the City' the ability to appreciate life and its variety, at a slightly aesthetic distance, is expressly put in terms of monied leisure:

> Had I but plenty of money, money enough and to spare,
> The house for me, no doubt, were a house in the city-square.
> Ah, such a life, such a life, as one leads at the window there!

So one may appreciate the detail of the fountain, and watch the arrival of the travelling doctor, a procession for Our Lady, and the Duke's guard bringing up the rear. The Duke's politics, however, would be of no interest: part of the world of clock time. In 'Love Among the Ruins' the narrator's girl awaits him in the ruined turret of a circus where once the king looked down on chariot racing, and beyond that on causeways and aqueducts. The substitution of girl for king is to Browning's liking; nor does the ruin of proud, ambitious busyness displease him: 'Love is best!'

The open-minded immersion in life is characteristic of the individual who accords the highest value to love. But it is also the basis of good art. Fra Filippo Lippi leaps over the wall of the friary and paints the varied life around him, rather than attempt some abstract version of the sacred (which, in a sense, is his *job*). As a result his works offer greater glory to God and His creation.

Browning is a key figure in the transmission of certain ideas about the higher hedonism from the Romantics to the aesthetic movement and ultimately to Bloomsbury: moments of intensity; art as conveying these; Italy as arena for art and intensity. It is true that Browning's strenuousness does not appeal to the next generation, nor does his relatively confident derivation of art from life. 'To burn always with this hard gem-like flame, to maintain this ecstasy, is success in life,' said Pater: 'success': the word is provocatively chosen. But for Pater art is one intensity among others, though superior to others because more refined and exquisite. Yet

Browning and aestheticism approach each other subtly: *Dorian Gray* bears more than a superficial resemblance to 'My Last Duchess'. For the former shows how morally ugly is a devotion to beautiful appearances devoid of love, while the latter suggests that there is something potentially deadening in the aesthetic impulse even when it is most subject to the ends of fidelity to life. By the time that he wrote *The Picture of Dorian Gray* (1890) Wilde had abandoned the Pater version of aestheticism; but he was thinking still about the mode of existence that would free humanity for the pursuit of individual self-development and the arts: it required leisure. *The Soul of Man Under Socialism* (1891) is uncompromising in its attitude to physical labour, despite, or perhaps because of, the fact that he had worked on Ruskin's road:

> There is nothing necessarily dignified about manual labour at all, and most of it is absolutely degrading. It is mentally and morally injurious to man to do anything in which he does not find pleasure, and many forms of labour are quite pleasureless activities, and should be regarded as such. . . . Up to the present, man has been, to a certain extent, the slave of machinery, and there is something tragic in the fact that as soon as man had invented a machine to do his work he began to starve. This, however, is, of course, the result of our property system and our system of competition.[21]

Wilde's 'Socialism', to which he here alludes, is no more than a means of organising mechanical production so that 'the individual' can get on with the pursuit of Beauty: 'the community by means of organisation of machinery will supply the useful things and . . . the beautiful things will be made by the individual.'[22]

The theorists of Bloomsbury may not be eminent Victorians. Yet they sound a note so familiar from the nineteenth century that one soon seizes their indebtedness to the Romantic tradition I have attempted to isolate. Clive Bell, in *Civilization* (1928), which is dedicated to Virginia Woolf, treats the theme in a familiar fashion:

> What is peculiar to civilized people is, in the first place, that they are capable of recognizing the value of knowledge as a means to exquisite spiritual states, and, in the second, that they esteem this value above any remote, utilitarian virtue. Beauty, of course, has no practical value whatever.[23]

There is, however, a piece of covert aggression, both against the more earnest kinds of Victorian discussion of culture and against twentieth-century technophiles: it consists in the use of the word 'civilization' itself as a synonym for cultivation. For this usage, which is slightly outmoded, suggests refined eighteenth-century polish, as against high seriousness; while at the same time it denies the title of cultivation to modern industrial society. He goes on to describe the arrangements for creating a 'civilization' in characteristically élitist fashion. For this part of his argument he draws on a tradition that goes back to Arnold's educated lover of culture, and beyond to Coleridge's 'Clerisy'. But the contrast this evokes with Coleridge's almost scholastic conception shows how far Bell and his generation have been influenced by aestheticism:

> If I were a tyrant I would abdicate immediately. But had I inherited along with power a taste for doing good, my ambition would be to civilize. As a first step to that end I would establish and endow a leisured class every member of which should have enough and no more.[24]

There would be a lower class, thinned out by deliberate 'depopulation', and rescued from absolute drudgery by labour-saving machines.[25] The work of Clive Bell, once influential chiefly through his essay on *Art* (1913), is less well known than it was, except for the survival of the term 'significant form' in aesthetics and the discussion of painting. But the formalism of that concept is itself closely dependent on the search for exquisitely pleasurable states of mind, which are held to be only possible for a few. When put in less overtly élitist terms the thesis still posits a connection between art and leisured people. Thus another Bloomsbury theorist, Roger Fry, in his essay on 'Art and Socialism': 'The Great State aims at human freedom; essentially, it is an organization for leisure – out of which art grows.'[26] It is worth distinguishing the Bloomsbury position from the comparably élitist Leavisite attitude to leisure and culture, expressed in F. R. Leavis and Denys Thompson, *Culture and Environment*:

> The modern labourer, the modern clerk, the modern factory-hand live only for their leisure, and the result is that they are unable to live in their leisure when they get it. Their work is meaningless to them, merely something they have to do in order

to earn a livelihood, and consequently when their leisure comes it is meaningless, and all the uses they can put it to come almost wholly under the head of what Stuart Chase calls 'decreation'.[27]

Here, despite the idea that one may use leisure well, the emphasis is on finding the right, creative, kind of labour.

What then are the qualities of the tradition I have been examining? I think it is possible to isolate several tendencies, which often occur together, from the broader currents I have also adumbrated: a vaguely organicist conception of time; the chief end in life as the experience of exquisitely pleasurable states of consciousness; the implicit or explicit idea of a leisured élite, free for the free play of consciousness out of which the good moments come, and able to enshrine or confect those moments in art. I suspect that it is a view which, *via* Bloomsbury, has been at least as influential on British cultural life until recently as the Leavisite one: on Bohemia; on painters and sculptors especially, who were prepared by Bell and Fry for the sorts of arguments that might be mounted in favour of abstract expressionism by a critic such as Clement Greenberg; and on the liberal Establishment, where Bell's use of the word 'civilization' could be heard in Roy Jenkins's call for 'the civilized society'. It is not a call which is heard now in any form from any section of the Establishment.

Notes

1. See for instance Raymond Williams, *Culture and Society 1780–1950* (Harmondsworth, 1961) pp. 50–51.
2. Thomas Blackwell, *An Enquiry into the Life and Writings of Homer* (London, 1735) p. 40.
3. Ibid., p. 84.
4. John Brown, *A Dissertation on the Rise, Union, and Power, the Progressions, Separations, and Corruptions, of Poetry and Music* (London, 1763) p. 39.
5. Adam Ferguson, *An Essay on the History of Civil Society*, 6th edn (London, 1793) p. 288.
6. Ibid., p. 290.
7. Ibid., p. 294.
8. Ibid., p. 296.
9. Quoted in Williams, op. cit., p. 52.
10. *Wordsworth's Poetical Works*, (ed.) Thomas Hutchinson, rev. E. de Selincourt (London, 1960) p. 953.
11. Quoted in Raymond Plant, *Hegel* (London, 1973) pp. 22–3.

12. See Goethe, *Dichtung und Wahrheit*, Book 1, *Sämtliche Werke*, (Berlin, 1902), Vol. 24, p. 81.
13. *The Complete Writings of William Blake* (London, 1972) p. 337.
14. Ibid., p. 593.
15. Ibid., p. 612.
16. Ibid., p. 526.
17. Matthew Arnold. *Culture and Anarchy with Friendship's Garland and Some Literary Essays* (Ann Arbor, 1965) p. 102.
18. Ibid., p. 105.
19. Alan Sinfield, *Alfred Tennyson* (Oxford, 1986) p. 50.
20. Richard Ellmann, *Oscar Wilde* (London, 1987) pp. 70–71.
21. *Complete Works of Oscar Wilde* (ed.) J. B. Foreman, intro. Vyvyan Holland (London and Glasgow, 1966) pp. 1088–9.
22. Ibid., p. 1089.
23. Clive Bell, *Civilization: An Essay*, 2nd edn (London, 1932) p. 92.
24. Ibid., p. 239.
25. Ibid., p. 240.
26. Roger Fry, *Vision and Design*, 3rd edn (Harmondsworth, 1937) pp. 68–9.
27. F. R. Leavis and Denys Thompson, *Culture and Environment: The Training of Critical Awareness* (London, 1933) pp. 68–9.
[References to poems, when not supplied, are to the relevant Oxford Standard Authors text, except in the case of Arnold, when they are to *The Poems of Matthew Arnold*, (ed.) K. Allott, (London, 1965).]

3

Up Tails All: Leisure, Pleasure and Paranoia in Kenneth Grahame's *The Wind in the Willows*

G.M. Hyde

Kenneth Grahame's children's classic is not hard to 'place', as F. R. Leavis used to say. Indeed, I recall a 'dating' seminar (as we quaintly used to call them) at Downing in which we presented him with the florid nature-poem in chapter 3, 'The Wild Wood' (the passage beginning 'Such a rich chapter it had been') assuming that he would not be able to recognise it; which he didn't; but he *did* tell us confidently that it was very 'ninetiesish, though later than the 'nineties, yes surely Edwardian. And *The Wind in the Willows* surely *is* Edwardian, in style, themes, ideology. The Edwardian period in English literary culture is short but distinctive,[1] and Kenneth Grahame, Secretary to the Bank of England and erstwhile contributor to the *Yellow Book*, had a special role in articulating its consciousness and prolonging its after-echoes in the popular imagination by means of one of the most frequently reprinted books in the English language.[2]

In saying what is Edwardian about this text one is inevitably taking on a considerable range of cultural and social phenomena, some of them altogether specific to the decline of Victorian literature as an institution, and some simply in the air, redolent in a very diffuse way of Imperialism in the beguiling guise of (as Lenin called it) a higher stage of Capitalism.[3] The bourgeois social order that sustained literature had become profoundly inward-looking, but it could not ignore either the premonitions of war or the need to confront the growth of an articulate proletariat.[4] The Arts and Crafts movement, Impressionism, and Symbolism (with its quasi-religious aesthetic and its mystical overtones) feed into Grahame's novel[5] alongside a rather despairing sense of the peculiar hypertrophy of the English class system, reflected elsewhere in Edwardian and early Georgian writing. Maybe there was a new-found leisure (for some) to think, or at least to ruminate; there was certainly hard-earned money (for some) to spend, during that short-lived holiday that preceded the First World War. Moreover, in response to a kind of post-industrial expansiveness, childhood was being constructed anew, not least by Grahame's earlier work.[6] For the post-Victorians it seems to have represented a continuing Golden Age, sweeping all that agony about virtue and faith, oppression and righteousness, along with other Victorian obsessions, under a rich Indian carpet[7] of leisure, pleasure, and adventure. All of this, and a lot more, is present in Grahame's bizarre Edwardian masterpiece.

It is chapter 7, above all, that 'places' *The Wind in the Willows* in the context of the literature of decadence, and supplies the cultural resonances that still shape our reading of the novel. The notably *ingénu* and insecure Mole, the book's most childlike (feminine?) character, incongruously recalls Mallarmé's Faun abandoned to his seemingly endless afternoon of desire, as he (Mole) lies 'stretched on the bank, still panting from the stress of the fierce day' (one of the novel's many colourful evocations of *dolce far niente*).[8] Grahame aligns himself here (as he did elsewhere in real life) with the bards of sensation for whom pleasure is work of heroic proportions (cf. Huysmans's Des Esseintes, or Baudelaire). Grahame's Edwardian dilution of nineties paganism (cf. Forster, Housman, even some of Lawrence) – in effect a middle class assimilation of late romanticism – finds magical expression in this chapter, the title of which was appropriated by Pink Floyd for a characteristically psychedelic album in 1967. Whenever, as here, the epic and picaresque (strongly plotted) Toad is out of the way, the story can regress quite happily to the lyrical state of arrest that is the mainstay of its dynamics in some burrow or leafy tunnel or other. Chapter 7 sets this tone at once by foregrounding an absent agent ('The Willow-Wren was twittering his thin little song, hidden himself in the dark selvedge of the river bank') and blurring all parameters of time and space: 'Though it was past ten o'clock at night, the sky still clung to and retained some lingering skirts of light from the departed day.'[9] – the anxious image of the withdrawal of the mother is characteristic. Time is arrested and spatialised before Mole's question: "You stayed to supper, of course?" said the Mole presently'.[10] – a reticent pause before 'presently' which there is no way of measuring, and which perfectly expresses the gentility of a society sure of its manners but anxious lest the rituals should not be observed.[11]

This is one side of Grahame's sensibility, but it is not the world in which Toad lives. His frenetic, improvised, manic-depressive narrative (his friends quite rightly suppose that he is ill) is without authentic subjectivity: which is why he so casually risks death and puts others so cold-bloodedly at risk with apparent impunity.[12] Mole's paranoid mind-style, on the contrary, which is also *mutatis mutandis* Rat's, is haunted by secret pain and grief, introjects objects of desire and fear, skirts mourning by a hair's breadth (especially in 'Dulce Domum'), and is eroticised by a death-wish which recurrently threatens its emotional balance and its good-natured velvet-smoking-jacketed exterior.[13] Grahame carefully excluded death from his tale, wilfully attempting to conceal the truth that the tale tells, namely that death, too, has its place in Arcady, since without it the transcendent experience of chapter 7 is unimagineable;[14] but little Portly Otter is nevertheless brought close up against the supreme mystery, that of which animals do not talk.[15] Rat's drifting *bateau ivre* penetrates to the heart of the Male Mystery, the Dark Father who is lord of life and death, and as we draw nearer to the inner sanctum the female presence fades away, helpless:

> Embarking again and crossing over, they worked their way up the stream in this manner, while the moon, serene and detached in a cloudless sky, did what she could, though so far off, to help them in their quest; till her hour came and she sank earthwards reluctantly, and left them, and mystery once more held field and river.[16]

On the dark side of the moon, then, lies the world of Pan, whose Dionysiac music Rat, being a poet, can hear, while Mole cannot. Pan's world is the world of 'the end, whatever it might be': the domain, in other words, of the absconded Father (no need to dwell in any detail on the tragic early death of Grahame's mother and his father's subsequent incurable depression, alcoholism, and – literal – remoteness; nor to underline the grim irony in the fate of the young Alastair for whom these pages were written).[17] The climax of the episode has a poignant inevitability: Portly searches 'like a lost child' for the absconded Pan-figure, the protector, then subsides in tears: whereupon 'the Mole ran quickly to comfort the little animal'. At times like these we are reminded of the vulnerability of the human–animal protagonists, and, through them, that we live in a fallen, post-heroic world in which our chief gift seems to be the leisure to contemplate our inadequacies (a distant echo of Baudelaire's 'héroisme de la vie moderne'.[18]) Rat rounds off the chapter with a neo-pagan poem that would not have discredited Swinburne, Johnson or Dowson:

> Lest the awe should dwell
> And turn your frolic to fret
> You shall look on my power at the helping hour
> But then you shall forget!
>
> Lest limbs be reddened and rent
> I spring the trap that is set
> As I loose the snare you may glimpse me there
> For surely you shall forget!
>
> Helper and healer, I cheer
> Small waifs in the woodland wet
> Strays I find in it, wounds I bind in it
> Bidding them all forget.[19]

We are at the gentler – and more genteel – end of the Rhymers Club and Yeats's 'Tragic Generation',[20] where a fusion of Christian and Hellenic elements articulates an endless, and of course hopeless, Long Vacation pursuit of pleasure; or those Edwardian weekends spent exploring the countryside (which in 1908 included among its charms, unmentioned by Grahame, wholesale unemployment and grinding poverty, together with the disastrous social and moral consequences of these).[21]

The sublunary world, however, when it is detached from its moments of vision, never loses touch with material values and good living. The twinkling star in the river bank, seen both by Mole and by Toad,[22] is the benign eye of Rat gazing out of his well-appointed quarters. Rat's poetry 'thing' is not overstressed; it is a pursuit a gentleman may be forgiven, provided he keeps it to himself and it does not interfere with the earthly bliss of just being carried along by the river of Life while the ducks dabble, up tails all. (The lines quoted above end not with a swoon but with a snooze.) Meals punctuate strenuous sequences of escape and inertia, and the table and the cooking pot serve as focal points of bonhomie and well-being in a world mostly contained within civilised limits. (The peripeteia of Mole's and Rat's early boating adventure is made to focus upon a hamper stuffed with mouth-watering concrete (oral) poetry: 'coldtonguecoldhamcoldbeefpickled-gherkinssaladfrenchrollscresssandwidges[sic]pottedmeatgingerbeer-lemonadesodawater').[23] Even Mole's frugal pantry furnishes a Christmassy feast (supplemented by the tuck-shop)[24] and Toad's horsey transgression is rewarded with a suitably transgressive plate of stew.[25] (Huck Finn notes that in a stew the flavours 'swap about': maybe Grahame is taking a holiday from Elspeth's frugal housekeeping, just as Huck does from his aunt's.)[26] The secret passage into Toad Hall lies through the butler's pantry.

House images compose a veritably Freudian nexus of associa-tions, displacements, introjection, and projection.[27] The leisure ethic or pleasure principle drives one irresistibly up and out and away from home, whether it is a snug burrow like Mole's or a grand family mansion (held by dubious moral right) like Toad's; but the pleasure of quitting domesticity in favour of life (while avoiding, if possible, the Wild Wood and the Wide World) is counterbalanced by strategies of rediscovery and return, so that what we are in fact witnessing all the time is some kind of Freudian 'Fort/Da' game.[28] In chapter 5, 'Dulce Domum', Mole is artfully made to encounter all over again the small inner space by which his real self has been constituted, sharing it willingly and con-vivially with Rat and some transient fieldmice, and, as it were, reconsecrating it with a couple of bottles of porter. Profoundly reassuring, too, is Badger's labyrinthine retreat, where things take on a harsher tonality but are nevertheless firmly under control. Badger lives at the heart of the Wild Wood, surrounded by animals who at best are 'not so bad really'.[29] His home speaks of (lost) Wisdom and (hard-pressed) Virtue built upon and within and against the secret ways of a great dead civilisation not unlike ours.[30] Badger himself, whose crusty gracelessness speaks of his authen-ticity, and who has an even more pronounced tendency to fall asleep than the other animals, is a cross between an eccentric housemaster and one of those Immortals (or Grahame's loved and hated Olympians) with their mysterious command of what is past and passing and to come. His Gothic Byzantium stands invulner-able at the very heart of Anarchy, strong because pure and absol-utely simple and honest: and if it is, in the end, yet another burrow that vulnerable animals can flee into, it nevertheless carries one safely back into one's own familiar territory: though by a devious subterranean route, to be sure.

Toad Hall is altogether more problematic. If Arnold and Pater are Grahame's presiding geniuses in this novel (I am leaving out of account for the time being the rich influence of Scott, Dumas etc.) then Toad seems to represent much of what Arnold diagnosed (with sadness and some foreboding) in the class he designated Barbarians.[31] Arnold had not the misfortune to live in the age of the internal combustion engine, or he would doubtless have added the motor car to his comprehensive definitions of the forces of Anarchy and the 'machinery' (he did not, of course, mean just the technical sort) that makes sweetness and light so hard to come by in our time. Toad represents the landed gentry, and as such is part of the hereditary ruling class of Barbarians (always following some field sport or devising unintellectual leisure activities as they are) that Arnold condemns, but with a sigh of nostalgia. Like Byron, that quintessential aristocrat, they have 'daring, dash and grandiosity'. But they also, like Byron, tend to live irregular lives. Motor cars represent both proclivities. Drawing, doubtless, upon Maeterlinck's essay 'On a Motor Car' (which also seems to have influenced Marinetti's celebrated raptures, a little later in time and in quite a different cultural ethos)[32] Grahame celebrates, through Toad, that which he condemns, thus subscribing very characteristically to both the narcissistic fear of change and the technological open-endedness of modernism. Maeterlinck puts it well:

> I give a slow turn to the mysterious 'advance-ignition' lever, and regulate carefully the admission of the petrol. The pace grows faster and faster, the delirious wheels cry aloud in their gladness. And at first the road comes moving towards me, like a bride waving palms, rhythmically keeping time to some joyous melody. But soon it grows frantic, springs forward, and throws itself madly upon me, rushing under the car like a furious torrent, whose foam lashes my face; it drowns me beneath its waves, it blinds me with its breath![33]

Maeterlinck writes of cars in an idiom (glamorous and ironic) that would now find acceptance only in advertisements, especially television commercials: and Grahame, as a good Edwardian, evidently felt some of this same thrill at possessing one's own fantasy-machine that could conquer time and space (cf. section 6 of Maeterlinck's essay: whimsical on the surface, but very serious underneath). The devastation of Toad's caravan by the rampant, anonymous, here-and-gone motor car is as compelling an image of the profound ambiguity of modernity as Hardy's Titanic.[34]

And Toad Hall therefore becomes a pregnant and complex symbol. It is an Ancestral House, steeped in the bitterness of power, like those of which Yeats wrote, and which he loved so equivocally. It is Forster's Howard's End or Lawrence's great houses (Shortlands, Breadalby, Wragby) which embody the Arnoldian myth of inheritance (tradition and the individual talent, or the cultural and social function of élites) as well as pointing sadly to the changed circumstances which make their hegemonic claims (founded, it should be said, on a range of different and partly irreconcilable premises) so hard to sustain. Toad Hall runs, as Grahame wryly observed, without servants;[35] yet of course to be in service in such a house, or even a poor imitation of it, was a viable way of life for a significant proportion of the work-force before the First World War; and after the war there was classic dismay that servants were either unobtainable or cripplingly expensive. The Barbarian Toad shows no inclination to betray his class: he treats the Populace (Arnold's term) with casual hauteur, and can talk his way round the solid representatives of the Philistines, Rat, Mole and Badger, without difficulty, since he constantly breaks the rules of virtue which they endorse (and seems to sense that the other animals do not always invoke them with entire conviction). As Badger points out, Toad's father was a sensible animal, and Toad is unworthy of him (his class is in decline). It has fallen to the solid middle classes, or those members of the middle classes who can find 'spontaneity of consciousness' to supplement 'strictness of conscience' (Arnold), to shoulder the burden of Improvement whereby whatever was valuable in the old order of things can be carried forward into Modern Times (with all the equivocation that such a formula is bound to produce – produced, indeed, in Arnold's own work).

Toad Hall, we know, is part fourteenth-century;[36] that is, it belongs to human history, unlike the residences of the 'aliens' (again, Arnold's term for those who cannot accept uncritically the values of their class seems very appropriate) – namely, Rat, Mole and Badger. Toad exposes himself recklessly to human law and human judgement (though he escapes each time with impunity).

He squanders his inheritance, he shows himself delightfully indif-
ferent to his house while it is securely his, and then becomes very
anxious about it (though powerless to do anything to repossess it)
when it falls into the hands of the (class) enemy: he is not drawn
back home, like Mole, by an irresistible elective affinity. It is not
Toad, but the alien Philistines Rat, Mole and Badger (the new
bourgeois intelligentsia, with luck) who care enough about the
values represented by Toad Hall to want to reinstate Toad as Lord
of the Manor (though one might have thought that they would
have had enough of him), have the energy and skill to do it, and by
doing so preserve the status quo. Although this is never said (it
could not be articulated at the allegorical level) the Terrible Three
(whose assault on Toad Hall turns them into parody Musketeers)
care more that the symbolic Ancestral House should not fall to the
Weasels and the Stoats than that Toad should be restored in all his
glory. Indeed, the 'change of heart' that their stern code of virtue
keeps demanding of Toad, and which he constantly thwarts,
almost seems to have been realised by the end: it is indeed a sunset
glow that sees the restored Toad renouncing, with scarcely any
pressure being applied, his deep urge to sing songs and tell tales of
his prowess (though he will doubtless be arrested *any day now* for
his criminal conduct). With Toad back where he belongs, the world
is safe for the Moles and the Rats, secure from the depredations of
the Weasels and the Stoats (though to put it like this underlines the
fact that there is only one Mole, one Rat and one Badger: they will
remain without progeny). The Wild Wood, and the Wide World,
have been thrust back to a safe distance.

Toad Hall is not a 'personalised' (animalised) inner space like the
other residences in the novel. Even in his account of it to the
all-too-human Jailor's Daughter, Toad uses house-agents' jargon
('eligible', forsooth[37]) rather than giving (until prompted) any real
idea of its meaning *for him*. As an extension of his psyche, it
emphasises the fact that he is not comfortable in his own skin, a
fact that is everywhere apparent in his succession of manic crazes.
Like Toad himself, it is both grandiose and easily trespassed upon.
It is also relatively easily repossessed by three animals who, because
they are fit to be inheritors, seem to the representatives of the
populace to be as strong as an army. The chapter in which this
occurs, chapter 12, is called, with singular inappropriacy, 'The
Return of Ulysses'. There are no suitors, of course; only weasels
and stoats. There is no Telemachus (though it is interesting that

Toad, unlike the Oedipal aliens who have slain the Father, is known to have had a father who was his moral superior, and is remembered – and celebrated – by Badger). And above all there is no Penelope, because the world of this novel is a club which women may not enter. But there *is* a sort of bourgeois epic being written in and around these closing pages, and one which more than endorses the trust Arnold vested in the educated bourgeoisie and their spontaneous Hellenism. The Edwardian age was an age of very real democratisation: the spectre of which Marx and Engels spoke was haunting Europe:[38] but when all was said and done, the populace were (luckily) a disorganised lot – nothing but a 'mob', in fact, and 'anarchic' in a more specific sense[39] – and the enlightened but traditionalist middle classes, taking over whatever remained inspirational and vital from the aristocratic ethos, would easily demonstrate that mass man was an ideological chimera when confronted by liberal individualism. The classicising that keeps breaking out throughout the narrative, redolent of public school prep., comes in handy here to dignify a playground brawl or 'king of the castle' game. Grahame was, of course, by no means the first to link the classics with sport or leisure in this way, nor the last.[40]

The influence of *The Wind in the Willows* in English culture is literally incalculable. Even discounting A. A. Milne's popular but rather opportunist adaptation for the stage, *Toad of Toad Hall*, wherein all the secret places of Grahame's tormented soul are either simply written out or shut away from the public gaze in favour of an (almost exclusive) two-dimensional Toadian plot, Grahame's book has reached an enormous audience. (80,000 copies a year is no mean achievement.) Evidently, it cannot lay claim to the intellectual brilliance of *Alice*, and it has probably penetrated less far beyond the boundaries of Great Britain than the adventures of Pooh Bear.[41] Moreover, though tempting, it would be fatuous to try to assess its audience by drawing comparisons with the products of contemporary popular culture, though one might guess at the way certain cartoon animals (owing very little to E. H. Shepard's rather rebarbative and troubling drawings) have found their inspiration in Grahame's riverbank and wood. But *The Wind in the Willows* does seem to be irreplaceable, at least in the English-speaking world, and some informed conjectures as to the reason for this might be in order. Grahame's treatment of Nature would have to come high on the list of reasons: *The Wind in the Willows* manages to combine a kind of Darwinist thesis about the survival of the fittest with a sentimental but quite genuine love of Mother Nature. If this is a contradiction, it is one which continues to inform the mind of the English middle classes in the age of the greenhouse effect, as the media confirm daily. As to animals, it is pretty obvious that there aren't any in the book; but a corollary of this is that the book is in fact not sentimental about animals except when it is being sentimental for other reasons. The games it plays with class attitudes are transparent and thoroughly English: despite the tendentious treatment of the Wild Wooders, the upshot is at worst a bit patronising and at best reassuring to those who, willy-nilly, line up alongside Rat and Mole in the school playground and wonder why these two amiable animals have put up with Toad for as long as they have. Like Arnold, Grahame belongs with the reformed and spiritualised middle classes who were busy devising and perpetuating the grammar-school model of an intellectual élite open to the talents, but in touch with the aristocratic virtues which still maintained an unaccountable superiority. And if we are beginning, in our anarchic age, to wonder what, if anything, will continue to speak to generations to come about the river banks that have survived the theme park as well as the motorway, secret places nurturing the knowledge of a personal and intimate kind that is the quintessence of the fine art of leisure and will have no truck with what Lawrence called 'the plausible ethics of productivity', Grahame's classic may provide some important answers.

Notes

1. Recent attempts to define it include S. Hynes, *The Edwardian Turn of Mind* (Oxford, 1968), J. Hunter, *Edwardian Fiction* (London, 1982) and J. Batchelor, *The Edwardian Novelists* (Cambridge, Mass., 1982).
2. Peter Green, in his excellent critical biography *Kenneth Grahame: 1859–1932* (London, 1959), mentions a figure of 80,000 copies a year. There is a familiar irony in the fact that Bodley Head initially turned it down, and that early reviews contrasted it unfavourably with *The Golden Age*.
3. V. I. Lenin's *Imperialism: A Higher Stage of Capitalism* was first published in 1916.
4. It is often said that the foundations of the Welfare State were laid by the social reforms of the first decade of the century, especially in association with the Liberal landslide of 1906. (The National Insurance Act of 1911 was particularly significant.) But as Green points out, Grahame was very familiar with William Morris's work, in which a

powerful (even Marxist) egalitarianism is combined with Arts and Crafts communitarian aestheticism.

5. Cf. Mark Girouard, *The Return to Camelot: Chivalry and the English Gentleman* (Yale, 1981). Girouard's primary topic is the cultural use and abuse of the Arthurian theme, but he also communicates a vivid sense of Edwardian attitudes and styles generally.

6. Grahame wrote regularly for the *National Observer* and occasionally for other publications, including the *Yellow Book*; but his early, much-admired tales of childhood, with their strong elements of idealisation and romance, and the privileged space, privacy, and inwardness of upper-middle-class life, are to be found, for the most part, in *The Golden Age* (1895) and *Dream Days* (1899).

7. There is an unmistakeable affinity between Grahame's world and E. M. Forster's, especially in *A Passage to India*.

8. Cf. Stephane Mallarmé, *L'Après-Midi d'un faune*, (1876). Like *The Wind in the Willows*, and much Symbolist writing, Mallarmé's poem is a typical closed system threatened by infinite regression.

9. Kenneth Grahame, *The Wind in the Willows*, (London, 1971) p. 126. All subsequent quotations are from this (the standard) edition.

10. Ibid., p. 127.

11. There are a number of tactful silences of a very British kind (e.g. in ch. 1, when the Otter suddenly leaves Rat and Mole in mid-sentence: 'The Rat hummed a tune, and the Mole recollected that animal-etiquette forbade any sort of comment on the sudden disappearance of one's friends at any moment, for any reason or no reason whatever.') This pregnant silence may be associated with the (non) appearance of Death in the riverbank idyll: 'An errant May-fly swerved unsteadily athwart the current in the intoxicated fashion affected by young bloods of May-flies seeing life. A swirl of water and a "cloop!" and the May-fly was visible no more. Neither was the Otter.' Mayflies epitomise the brevity of life.

12. Very little, at times, distinguishes Toad from a common criminal who goes unpunished only because he is who he is. Such things are not unknown in public life.

13. Toad is, broadly speaking, to Mole as the manic-depressive position is to the paranoid. Laplanche and Pontalis, *The Language of Psycho-Analysis:* (London, 1983) note (following Klein) that the depressive (or manic-depressive) position supersedes the paranoid position in the middle of the first year of life, as soon as the child is able to apprehend the mother as a whole object. 'The splitting of the object into a "good" and "bad" object is attenuated, with libidinal and hostile instincts now tending to focus on the same object . . . the gap between the internal phantasy object and the external object is narrowed . . . ambivalence is thus established in the full sense of the word.' Toad experiences this stage as trauma (caravans, for example, are supremely good and irredeemably bad) but he *does* in a sense 'go through' it; and the return of Toad Hall constitutes a sort of reparation (at the end of a protracted phase of manic behaviour which invites punishment). Mole, on the other hand, suffers delusions of persecution, wherein the Wild Wood

seems to equate with castration. (It is trackless and, after the snow, without markers.) He is intensely oral, discovering the mother's breast everywhere, and much given to introjection of the idealised object; to deal with his anxiety, which threatens to engulf him, he resorts, in paranoid style, to disavowal (i.e. there is no threat, if we are successful in ignoring it) and omnipotent control (which explains his effective but otherwise out-of-character ploy in respect of the repossession of Toad Hall). Kenneth Grahame was five when his mother died: but it is worth pointing out that in the first year of his life his father changed his job, which involved moving, and the family lived in temporary accommodation for a full three years. Kenneth's first memory was of a railway journey (cf. Green). His love of tranquillity, combined with the powerful imagery of change and movement in *The Wind in the Willows*, doubtless originate in this first year of life in association with the unresolved manic-depressive and paranoid stages of development.

14. Green is illuminating on Grahame's relationship with Richard Jefferies, not least in the matter of attitudes to death, which Jefferies unequivocally locates at the heart of the natural cycle.

15. The 'dark father' turns out to be a stern but kindly protector of the natural order.

16. The manic-depressive and paranoid positions are of course formative stages in the development of the Oedipus Complex. A similar regressive boat journey is the subject/'story' of Rimbaud's *Le Bateau ivre* (1883).

17. The sad tale is well told by Green, though the intensity of Alastair's depression remains something of a mystery.

18. Like Baudelaire, Grahame was (in part, at least) a dandy who strove to live by the courage of his affectations.

19. *The Wind in the Willows*, p. 141. The poem is woven into the text, as if to assimilate or efface it.

20. Cf. W. B. Yeats, *The Tragic Generation*, in *Autobiographies* (London, 1914).

21. Cf. Rider Haggard, *Rural England* (London, 1902).

22. *The Wind in the Willows*, p. 10; ibid., p. 210.

23. Ibid., p. 13.

24. Ibid., pp. 97–102.

25. Ibid., pp. 200–1.

26. Mark Twain, *Huckleberry Finn*.

27. Lawrence said that one 'sheds one's sicknesses in books'. If Grahame's novel can be called escapist, it nevertheless digs deep into the self-divisions of a psyche (and arguably a representative modern psyche).

28. Cf. Sigmund Freud, *Beyond the Pleasure Principle* (London, 1922).

29. *The Wind in the Willows*, p. 81.

30. Cf. Richard Jefferies, *After London* (1885). Peter Green comments on Grahame's extensive debt to Jefferies.

31. Matthew Arnold, *Culture and Anarchy* (1869).

32. Maurice Maeterlinck, 'On a motor car', in *The Double Garden* (London, 1904). Maeterlinck undoubtedly influenced F. T. Marinetti, the Italian

Futurist, who, in his *Founding Manifesto of Futurism* (Milan, 1909), apotheosises the racing car, paying numerous tributes elsewhere to the pleasures of motoring.

33. Maurice Maeterlinck, op. cit., p. 147.
34. Thomas Hardy, *The Convergence of the Twain* in *Satires of Circumstance*, (London, 1914).
35. Cf. Peter Green, op. cit.
36. *The Wind in the Willows*, p. 146.
37. Ibid.
38. Karl Marx and Friedrich Engels, *The Manifesto of the Communist Party* (1848).
39. Cf. Arnold on the Hyde Park Riots, op. cit.
40. Thomas Hughes, *Tom Brown's Schooldays* (1857) inaugurated a whole genre of 'mock-classical' writing, which then assimilated other heroic stereotypes.
41. There is, for example, a Pooh Bear Street in Warsaw, and Frederick Crews's volume of literary critical parodies *The Pooh Perplex* (London, 1979); but Grahame is all too often represented abroad by *Toad of Toad Hall*, a very different kettle of fish from *The Wind in the Willows*.

4

P. G. Wodehouse: The Case of Leisure as the Sole Topic of an Author's Output

S. J. S. Ickringill

For those of us who first came to Wodehouse through the medium of Penguin Paperbacks, certain glowing critical comments on the book covers stick in the mind. The endlessly repeated encomium by Waugh is not the most apposite here, however (for those who feared another repeat). Probably the most relevant on the occasion of one more, rather solemn discussion of Wodehouse's work is that of A. P. Ryan in the *New Statesman*, quoting the assertion in Punch that trying to criticise Wodehouse is like taking a spade to a soufflé. Wodehouse was amused, perhaps a little irritated, by those who examined his work with critical zeal. He referred even to the magnificent Richard Usborne as 'a certain learned Usborne'.[1] When, as is often the case on scholarly occasions, footnotes are added by way of paraphernalia, then Wodehouse's now heavenly ridicule is assured.[2] Clearly unease is an appropriate sensation for anyone trying to say something 'serious' about the work of an immensely able, if self-consciously limited, comic writer.[3] Why spoil a good thing? After all, Wodehouse certainly had no message. Wodehouse was of the view that writing was to be enjoyed, not analysed. His own writing was the product of enormous hard work directed towards the amusement of his readers.

The essential point is that Wodehouse protested too much. Of course he wrote about life as if it was a musical comedy and not 'the real thing', but there is a message to be discovered. An important part of that message is discussed in this essay. Pelham Grenville Wodehouse, an exceptionally hard-working man, wrote almost entirely about leisure. He discussed work to ridicule it.

52

Many of his favourite characters parodied work. The workers, his villains to the extent that he went in for such things, were ludicrous whether pig-men or publishers. Of course the drones were also thoroughly amusing, but they were usually equipped with a heart in the right place – unlike pig-men or publishers, not to mention at least some Hollywood producers and the odd Broadway impressario. The pervasiveness of leisure, as the topic of his writing, combined with something like hostility to work, can be discussed in terms of Wodehouse's own life and the context in which he lived and worked. It is intended to develop this theme both by wide ranging references and by concentrating on one novel that Wodehouse himself said was a considerable favourite of his.[4]

Wodehouse had a major and much picked over disaster in his life when he made a series of broadcasts from Berlin during the war.[5] There had been an earlier disaster, much more private, but one that had a profound effect on the young writer. Wodehouse, like his admired brother Armine before him, was enjoying himself hugely at Dulwich, and hoped to follow Armine to Oxford. Pelham was a good classicist (a gifted versifier in Greek and Latin, much given to parody). Just as importantly the younger Wodehouse was a useful cricketer, boxer and rugby player. Turn-of-the-century Oxford might have been designed for such a man. Then it became obvious that his father could not afford to send him in his brother's footsteps. Predictably enough Wodehouse dealt with this calamity good humouredly, at least in retrospect. What had happened was clearly outside his or anyone else's control. 'The authorities' paid his father's pension (his father had been a judge in Hong Kong) in rupees. This was a coinage of uncertain moods and markedly unstable. This instability put paid to an Oxford career for Wodehouse. The mechanisms which caused such disasters to occur were mysterious and certainly beyond Pelham's understanding. They were to remain so. Indeed, as the young Wodehouse was successfully urged to go and work in the Lombard Street branch of the Hong Kong and Shanghai Bank, mystification increased.

In his letters and slightly less obviously in his creative writing Wodehouse made fun of all of this experience. He kept coming back to it.[6] Banking was beyond comprehension – part of the same mysterious world as the eccentric rupee. 'If there was a moment in the course of my banking career when I had the foggiest notion of what it was all about, I am unable to recall it.'[7] Not least because of this direct personal experience Wodehouse tended to see all conventional work as either inexplicable or tedious, or both (perhaps an accurate enough perception). Fixed Deposits and Inward Bills were impenetrable. Yet, we must not let Wodehouse sweep us along quite so happily and unquestioningly. There was nothing inevitable about a public school product finding banking impossible to understand. Wodehouse was, after all, a good classicist and in his time such a background was commonplace among successful bankers. Essentially Wodehouse did not want to understand.

Partly this can be explained in entirely personal terms. Wodehouse did know what he wanted to spend his life doing and that was writing. As a schoolboy writer, young writer, mature writer, elderly writer and remarkably elderly writer he worked very hard indeed. But this was not real work, for it was an activity Wodehouse loved. In addition he knew what it was to work on his left jab or his front foot technique. Writing was to be the fundamentally important thing for him, but he also worked at essentially leisure activities, as did so many of his contemporaries. Wodehouse was lucky enough to enjoy his work, so it ceased to be work as the term was conventionally understood, not least by Wodehouse. By definition, work was something distasteful. Banking came to mind as an example.

This answer, essentially one based on Wodehouse's very personal experience, is incomplete. There is much in Wodehouse's attitude that is far from being unique to him. After all, should a gentleman work – could a gentleman work without losing caste? For those with a public-school background, even a fairly modest one such as Dulwich, such problems were real enough. After all, commonly enough at Wodehouse's beloved Dulwich, boys were likely to have parents in Trade or Commerce, possibly even in Industry. At school the ethos of the amateur was dominant. More than just the amateur ethos was in the ascendant, the ethos of amateur gentlemanly effortlessness was pervasive. Not only did young men have doubts about going on to work in a mundane job, but even success in important things like games should be achieved with an air of effortlessness. The more scholarly boy might be acceptable, but not if he was obviously a swot. The point can best be developed by reference to Wodehouse's most famous creations, Jeeves and Bertie.[8]

Bertie is the definitive Drone, and an Old Etonian at that, but he has his rivals. They range from Catsmeat Potter-Pirbright to Freddie

Widgeon. In between there are a legion of Eggs, Beans and Crum-
pets. They wore spats. Bertie did not need to work, in American
terms he was a 'coupon clipper', and he did not choose to work –
however frequently his Aunt Agatha might describe him as a
wastrel. He was no physical degenerate however. Characters with
whom Wodehouse wants us to have sympathy, however amused
that sympathy, rarely are. They are usually rather energetic, not to
say modestly gifted at some game or other. Lest it be thought that
Bertie's greatest gift was as a thrower of cards into a top hat in
rivalry with fellow members of The Drones, it is worth saying that
he was useful with a racquet in his hand. He had won a half blue
for squash. He could play tennis well enough to outclass curates at
his Aunt Agatha's country residence, although it has to be admitted that his golf was never really impressive. The long-lived
schoolboy in Wodehouse warmed to the athletically able hero who
would be properly modest about his abilities. As late as 1973, when
Bachelors Anonymous was published, we discover that Joe Pickering
was a champion amateur middleweight boxer. Bertie, unlike his
creator, was no boxer, but he was slim and agile – even athletic.

How agile Jeeves was we cannot be entirely certain, or, indeed,
how slim. He was 'a kind of darkish sort of respectful Johnnie', but
Wodehouse never goes into great particulars.[9] Indeed in *Jeeves
Takes Charge* we rapidly learn the key to Wodehouse's portrayal of
the character, and the basis for the development of that character.
Jeeves moves effortlessly from one place to another, bringing
healing balm or at least his own hang-over cure. He has to repeat
this activity many times. Yet Jeeves does work, he must have
worked. All we hear is of his messing about with things, not least
when packing – invariably impeccably. He could buttle with the
best of them when an emergency arose, although he was a gentleman's personal gentleman by preference. In some sense Jeeves
was a gentleman. He worked, he was a servant, and yet he did not
seem to do so. Essentially, for the purpose of the stories and
novels, he ran a Mayfair consultancy, solving the problems of
Bertie, his friends and relations. Whether it was this cerebral
activity or the more mundane aspects of his job, Jeeves continued
his triumphs with no obvious effort. As we have seen, he did not
seem to walk from place to place – he shimmered and was suddenly among those present. Jeeves out of breath, Jeeves sweating,
Jeeves with polish on his hands, are unthinkable. In 1905 Sir
Stanley Jackson captained the England cricket team against Australia

in all the Tests, won the toss on each occasion, led his team to a 2–0 series win, and topped both the batting and the bowling averages. All this by a man who only fitted in one full first-class season into his busy life, and never found the time to go on an overseas tour. Jeeves, officially a working servant, was in the Jackson mould. He was ridiculously good at his chosen task, and a great many other things as well.

There are no suggestions here that there are parallels with Wodehouse's Mike Jackson.[10] It is important to note, however, that there are pertinent things to be said about Mike's friend Psmith. Psmith was extraordinarily languid and very hostile to work, whether Banking or the Fish Trade.[11] He also talked dazzlingly well, apparently from infancy onward. His personal appearance was irreproachable and his sense of style considerable if idiosyncratic. He was a particularly determined maintainer of the view that most work is a distasteful necessity which nobody in his right mind would ever dream of performing unless forced to do so by some financial catastrophe.[12] It can be added that the financial catastrophe is likely to be largely inexplicable to the sufferer (usually a son, daughter, nephew or niece). Psmith is important in himself and in understanding Bertie and Jeeves because he eventually became Bertie and Jeeves. Psmith was both an inconsequential prattler and a doer of great things. He could manipulate those around him into providing a happy ending, and appear near certifiable. In the long run it proved much funnier to split him into two, but his view of leisure and work was inherited by Wooster and his man.

If there is plenty of evidence in Psmith-centred stories, and even more in those in which Bertie and Jeeves dominate proceedings, of a consistent view of work and leisure, there is arguably even more evidence when the noble walls of Blandings appear on the Shropshire skyline. (Indeed, *Leave it to Psmith* takes the great man to Blandings.) The leading servant at the Castle, Sebastian Beech the Butler, essentially adds tone to the proceedings. He even has enough presence to make a stately procession of one. Unlike Jeeves he is much given to bodily suffering, not least because he is so overweight. None the less, even Beech has to have an athletic past, albeit as a youthful cyclist. In his time at Blandings Beech has much to do, and his tasks include feeding the Empress when purloined for some good reason. He does such work with a heavy heart, but with the realisation that it is in the interests of young love. He is happiest when thoroughly at his leisure, preferably in his pantry sipping port and reading the doings of the less reputable sections of High Society. If those doings include reference to the Hon. Galahad Threepwood, then satisfaction is complete.

Galahad Threepwood, brother to the master of Blandings, the Earl of Emsworth (not, of course, master of anything when one of his sisters is in residence), is much admired by the younger members of the family and in the Servants' Hall. Gally has manifestly never had a job in his life and never does any work as such, although he does write his memoirs. Gally is indestructible. 'It was a standing mystery to all who knew him that one who had such an extraordinarily good time all his life should, in the evening of that life, be so superbly robust.'[13] He survives as best a younger son can, and spends a fair amount of time at Blandings, aiding his brother and infuriating his sisters. They see him as a blot on the family escutcheon, but they, and particularly Lady Constance, are clearly the villains of the piece. It is Galahad's intention to see their daughters or nieces married to unsuitable young men (usually good at games), or their sons and nephews to unsuitable young women (preferably connected with the theatre). He had spent a little time in South Africa when banished there by his father, the eighth Earl, because Gally wished to marry Dolly Henderson, magnificent in pink tights. He is determined that others will not be similarly bullied. Usually the young man in question has to be given enough money by the ninth Earl to enable him to buy an onion soup bar or a share in a Health Spa. The same approach goes for young men in the family who want to marry chorus girls – above all if they want to marry Sue Brown, Dolly Henderson's daughter by Jack Cotterleigh of the Irish Guards. Ronnie Fish, son of Lady Julia Fish, relict of Sir Miles Fish, is the man in love with Sue, and in Ronnie we have something of a star in the galaxy of those who pursue the leisured life. One can say this with confidence because his mother tells us so, and she includes a wider circle in her remarks. Addressing that Napoleon of Publishing, the first Lord Tilbury, she says 'My dear man no member of my family has ever shown any aptitude for anything except eating and sleeping.'[14] She further affronts Lord Tilbury by pointing out that he must give a job to Ronnie to take his mind off Sue Brown. It is a telling point, but Lord Tilbury is unmoved.

If Ronnie Fish is a star, how can Stanley Featherstonehaugh Ukridge be described? Ukridge S. F. was superbly idle. He was always hoping that something big would turn up, and predictably enough he had an aunt living in Wimbledon who sometimes supported him. For the most part he begged, even stole, from friends such as George Tupper who was something in the Foreign Office or from his friend Corky and his rather literary and theatrical circle. Indeed, when we meet this circle, there is something of the life of Wodehouse the ambitious young writer in early Edwardian London – not least the gatherings in cheap Soho restaurants. For the most part nobody has a bean. Some are working, and working hard, but not Ukridge. He has the big, broad outlook and he wants others to share it. In reality he spends a lot of time in bed planning, before sagging back exhausted. He is a man of wrath, and a great creation. Of course he is a gentleman or at least, as Richard Usborne emphasises, he is treated as such, and with great deference, by the ex-butler Bowles.[15] The Ukridge short stories give us one particularly quirky and perhaps unexpected kind of drone,[16] while the Mr Mulliner stories give a galaxy of minor drones, some of whom are full Drones. The choice includes Archibald Mulliner, who secured the affection of Aurelia Cammarleigh by his capacity to imitate hens, Mordred Mulliner, a poet and pyromaniac (a bit of an exaggeration, but defensible) and Roland Moresby Attwater, a rising essayist and critic, but one who had a bit of money as well. There was even the Hollywood connection for the Mulliner clan. Here one points with particular pride to Wilmot Mulliner, a distant connection of the sage of the Bar Parlour. Wilmot was a nodder.

> Putting it as briefly as possible, a Nodder is something like a Yes-Man, only lower in the social scale. A Yes-Man's duty is to attend conferences and say 'Yes'. A Nodder, as the name implies, is to nod. The chief executive throws out some statement of opinion, and looks about him expectantly. This is the cue for the senior Yes-Man to say yes. He is followed in order of precedence, by the second Yes-Man or Vice-Yesser, as he is sometimes called – and the junior Yes-Man. Only when all the Yes-Men have yessed, do the Nodders begin to function. They nod.[17]

Wodehouse may not have understood banking, but he had a firm handle on Hollywood.

These examples can be multiplied, and, among other possibilities, we have not touched on any 'Oldest Member' stories – all those young men who are something-in-the-city but play golf all day.[18] Multiplication would also involve qualification here and there. In Lord Emsworth's view good secretaries who 'work' for him at Blandings are those who do little and make him do less, unlike the Efficient Baxter who plagues him so. None the less, women seem something of an exception. We are clearly meant to approve of Eve Haliday's wish to do an honest day's work cataloguing the Blandings Library, despite Psmith's desire to monopolise her, in *Leave it to Psmith*. In *Bachelor's Anonymous* we find Sally Fitch replying to the question of whether or not she liked work with a very definite affirmative.[19] Generally speaking women were really very different from men.[20] However, rather than constant flitting in search of evidence, it is time to settle on a more sustained discussion of *Sam the Sudden*.

Sam the Sudden could be categorised as one of Wodehouse's 'light novels', although there are passages of characteristically well sustained farce. Wodehouse the sentimentalist is there, as well as the dazzling farceur. The author's fondness for this novel obviously has much to do with its setting, Valley Fields, his fictional version of Dulwich. There is a rather touching moment in his introduction to the 1972 edition when he notes that he has not seen Dulwich for thirty-three years. It was obviously an important book for Wodehouse, and it repays some scrutiny.

Sam Shotter is our hero. The novel, like so many other works by Wodehouse the inveterate transatlantic traveller, begins in New York before moving to London. In an office building on Upper Broadway Sam is not working, at least not at the job his uncle is employing him to do. He is organising, however. He is in charge of the Office Boys' High-Kicking Championship. The idea came to him when he saw one office boy 'practising kicks against the wall of a remote corridor' while he, Sam, had been 'wandering about his office in a restless search for methods of sweetening an uncongenial round of toil'.[21] His uncle and employer, John B. Pynsent, is not out of town as supposed and Sam is caught in his promotional activities. This uncle is in no doubt as to what lies behind such behaviour by his nephew, a nephew who in a few months has so demoralised the office staff. 'The English public school is the curse of the age', he tells Sam.[22] Sam went to Wrykyn (essentially Dulwich College moved from the suburbs to a more remote spot) and was happy there. His father, an old boy of the same school, was a failure in business, and so Sam is doubly hurt and his uncle doubly sure of his analysis – along with a host of social and economic commentators then and since. John B. Pynsent promptly unloads Sam on to Lord Tilbury, on the other side of the Atlantic. Lord Tilbury wants a favourable business deal out of Pynsent, and so will tolerate the imposition. That is how people get jobs in Wodehouse novels.

If there is a hint about Sam of Wodehouse himself at this early stage, Sam quickly becomes Bill Townend in his method of crossing the Atlantic. Townend had impressed his close school friend, indeed life-long friend, Wodehouse by going to sea in a tramp steamer, and it is in the tramp *Araminta* that Sam crosses the Atlantic, along with the incompetent ship's cook Clarence 'Hash' Todhunter. Townend was a constant in Wodehouse's life and the letters written for Townend are a major source for understanding Wodehouse the diligent writer. When Townend moved from the visual arts to writing himself, Wodehouse helped and encouraged.[23] After Sam's arrival in London he meets an old school friend Willoughby Braddock, the Bradder, who has always been much impressed by Sam's adventurous spirit. Wodehouse was impressed by Townend's courage and initiative, and not least by his sea story *The Tramp*. Needless to add, Sam has worked hard on the *Araminta*, doing a range of hard physical labour – although in an uneven, amateur way. He was, after all, playing at it.

Sam has a mission in life. It is to find a girl whose picture he has gazed at with increasing enthusiasm in a cabin he occupied while on a hunting trip. He is to find her in Valley Fields. Kay Derrick lives in the London suburbs because the family fortunes have collapsed. Col. Eustace Derrick of Midways Hall, Wiltshire had lost his money. He had been a too-trusting man. Kay thinks longingly of Midways, particularly at breakfast time when the calm and leisured morning meal at Midways seems so distant from the breakfasts eaten against the clock and the railway timetable by her uncle Mathew Wrenn, an editor in Lord Tilbury's empire. Her uncle has given her a home, and Kay is grateful and sensible, but she would dearly like to return to a more gracious life.

Before the plot matures in Valley Fields, Wodehouse reminds us that public school products are not automatically good things. Two doubtful products of the system behave badly. Bates and Tressider refuse to help Sam Shotter in a rather confused hour of need, and Bates (Claude Winngton-Bates to be fair and full) behaves unpleasantly towards Kay on at least two occasions. The failure of behaviour towards the old school companion occurs on the night of the Old Boys Dinner, which makes the incident particularly grave, while also allowing Wodehouse a gentle gibe at the worst excesses of school worship.[24] As far as Bates is concerned he was known to be a bounder at school, and so there is nothing surprising about his adult actions. Sam has had to chastise Claude Bates severely in his school days. There is little doubt that if boys failed certain tests at school, they would continue to do so throughout their adult lives.

Back in the mainstream of the story (essentially a romantic story), Sam discovers that having to work for Lord Tilbury has a compensation. Using his Pynsent-given power, Sam is able to insist that he should work with Kay's uncle Mathew on *Pyke's Home Companion*. Immediately and marvellously his work ceases to be work at all and becomes an agreeable game. He becomes Aunt Ysobel, an agony aunt, and dispenses advice to the lovelorn, including the faithful servant who has stayed with Kay after the wreck of her life in the country and of the county. With equal and proper inevitability Kay's servant, Claire Lippett, falls in love with, or at least becomes engaged to, 'Hash' Todhunter, Sam's dogged servant. Both 'Hash' and Claire come into the rather-useless-servant category, but they are loyal.

Other elements in the novel reinforce the main theme of my argument. It is in this book that we are introduced to Chimp Twist, Soapy Molloy and Dolly his wife. These are three American crooks, but crooks who, in the stories anyway, never succeed and are frankly incompetent. As is usually the case with Wodehouse, Dolly is the only one of the often warring trio who shows any ability in her chosen work. Generally Wodehouse found women more competent than men in his own life, ans so they appear in his creative work. Ethel Wodehouse, Pelham's wife, organised him with great energy.[25] Dolly does her best to organise the rather stately Soapy and to out-manoeuvre Chimp.

Chimp has a cover; he is J. Sheringham Adair, Private Detective. This means he spends some time in his office playing solitaire. The office setting helps the plot, and reminds us that a job is rarely real. Lord Tilbury, from the mighty office block opposite, turns up and gives Chimp an excuse to spend some time in Valley Fields, as do his opponents Soapy and Dolly. They are in pursuit of loot, and a very large amount of loot, stashed away in that idyllic suburb by a

burglar named Finglass. Fortunately Finglass's career is well
known to Mathew Wrenn's chess-playing partner Cornelius, estate agent, booster for his neighbourhood and local historian. With
Chimp unhappily reduced to the role of handyman in Sam's
household, there to keep an eye on Sam's love life on behalf of
Tilbury (troubled that John B. Pynsent will blame him if Sam
makes an unsuitable attachment), and with Soapy and Dolly determined to gain an entrance to Mon Repos, which our hero has
rented because it is next door to where Kay is staying with her
uncle, the Wodehousian complications of plot are moving to the
point of climax. Indeed, things are more complex than I have
suggested, but anything like a brief résumé of Wodehouse's met-
iculously worked out plots is never easy.

When Sam hears from Cornelius the story of Finglass and the
loot all becomes clear to him, and hopeful. He immediately grasps
that with the reward for the money (although he speculates about
keeping the lot) he will be in a position to marry Kay. Sam's
suggestion is buying a farm, perhaps on the Braddock estate near
Midways. However, lively goings-on interrupt his conversation,
notably Lord Tilbury, trouserless and angry. Soapy, who had his
trousers removed by Sam, has done the same to Tilbury. Of course
the code of behaviour is so strong that this device immobilises his
lordship as it has Soapy. A very angry Lord Tilbury tells Sam that
he has informed Pynsent of Sam's unsuitable attachment, and that
the deal which induced the head of the Mammoth Publishing
Company to give him a job is now not going through. Sam's uncle
is insisting that he return to the United States on the first available
boat (presumably, and preferably, a scheduled transatlantic liner).
Lord Tilbury observes, 'As I should imagine that a young man of
your intellectual attainments has little scope for making a living
except by sponging on his rich relatives, I presume that you will
accede to his wishes.' Shortly after this statement he adds that he
would not have employed Sam as an office boy, left to his own
devices.[26] Sam, who had earlier roundly abused Lord Tilbury for
his comments on Kay, now silences him by threatening to de-bag
him again. However, the harsh Lordly comments touch on a very
real problem for Sam. It is vitally necessary to find Finglass's swag
to make marriage a realistic possibility.

Kay lets Sam know that she will indeed marry him, worthless as
she is, when he tells her that he might as well return to the States
as there is no good reason to stay in England. Love is not a

problem, financial realities are. Mon Repos must be searched with massive determination. The problem is that, as Chimp Twist has found, there does not seem to be any loot, and it appears that Finglass was just a man with a nasty sense of humour. There is nothing beneath the floor of the top back bedroom of Mon Repos. Kay's response is that it does not matter as long as they have each other. Sam's response is to agree, however ridiculous he might have found the observation before he met Kay. But what are they to live on? Kay is confident that Sam will find a job, and she enthuses him. They agree that marrying on nothing will be a challenge, will be fun, will bring them even closer together. It is marvellous that Finglass's loot has proved to be chimerical, and that John B. Pynsent will disinherit his nephew. They muse on the awful case of a wealthy heir marrying an even wealthier heiress. They are sending themselves up, but their happy exaggerations are cut short by Mr Cornelius's insistence that he read them the relevant chapter of his definitive history of Valley Fields. All unknowing he then reveals that in Finglass's time Mon Repos and its neighbour San Rafael, the home of Kay and her uncle, were a single house called Mon Repos. Sam, asking him to repeat the information, exits upstairs in feverish haste. This time he is not frustrated. Soon he is staring at a parcel. 'With the look of a mother bending over her sleeping babe', he is looking at two million dollars. 'What', he asks, 'is ten per cent of two million?'[27] Kay and Sam, one presumes, are to enjoy their rural idyll somewhere near Midways. And who has made it possible, or rather, will make it possible? The money was stolen from the New Asiatic Bank, thin enough disguise for the Hong Kong and Shanghai. Just in case we were in any doubt as to how to view the New Asiatic/Hong Kong and Shanghai we had learnt as early as p. 79 that Lord Tilbury's sister had business to do in Lombard Street.

All ends well, as is proper. Sam and Kay are happy, so are Claire and 'Hash'. They are going to set up in a pub together, which is marvellous news for Willoughby Braddock because Claire's mother, who works for the Braddocks and bullies him unmercifully, is going to help them run it. Willoughby will be subject no longer to the exquisite humiliation of being addressed as 'Master' Willoughby in his own home, and of being told that he may not drink champagne. He proposes to go and have adventures in the way Sam used to, but, we guess, will do so no more. He announces that he is going to see the world. 'I'm going to be one of those fellows Kipling writes about.'[28]

P. G. Wodehouse had strong views on Rudyard Kipling. *Stalky and Co.* had a visible impact on him and on his own school stories.[29] He was a staunch defender of Kipling, and clearly thought he knew more about writing than most.[30] Pelham could come very close, and thoroughly untypically, to being angry on the subject.

> It's odd, this hostility to Kipling. How the intelligentsia do seem to loathe the poor blighter, and how we of the canaille revel in his stuff. One thing I do think is pretty unjust – when they tick him off for not having seen the future of the India Movement and all that sort of thing.[31]

Admittedly, in this letter, Wodehouse is irritated not just by George Orwell's criticism of Kipling (and, obviously, the criticism of a whole group, the dread 'intelligentsia') but by Orwell's misunderstanding of Wodehouse's own life and work. Wodehouse had been grateful for Orwell's support and encouragement over the whole Berlin disaster, but clearly the Old Etonian can be one of the enemy on occasion. Wodehouse disliked overtly literary men, and literary circles, and, though I doubt that he made any personal enemies in his life in the normal sense, he did become a controversial figure because of what he represented, or was seen to represent – very like Kipling. Of course controversy descended horribly and spectacularly on Wodehouse from the Berlin broadcasts onward, but it existed before. In 1939 the University of Oxford had awarded Pelham a Doctorate of Letters. Some were delighted, Waugh, Belloc and Compton Mackenzie for instance, others less so. They ranged from Sean O'Casey to E. C. Bentley. O'Casey's reaction was particularly angry and it is instructive to examine it. In 1941, in a letter to the *Daily Telegraph*, he refuses to lay emphasis on 'the poor man's babble in Berlin', but instead criticises 'the acceptance of him by a childish part of the people and the academic government of Oxford, dead from the chin up, as a person of any importance whatsoever in English humorous literature'.[32] In the same year he wrote to Gabriel Fallon that 'the civilisation that could let Joyce die in poverty, and crown with a Litt.D. a thing like Wodehouse, deserves fire and brimstone from heaven, and it is getting it.'[33] O'Casey is infuriated by Belloc's enthusiasm for Wodehouse, which he again contrasts with the treatment received by Joyce.

There is much to be said here, not least about the way that Wodehouse became involved in the great debate over modernism.

For the purposes of my argument, however, O'Casey's reference to 'the childish part of the people' is helpfully provocative. It is not a simple left–right division of opinion. Orwell, for all his criticism of Wodehouse, recognised his ability, O'Casey really did thoroughly despise Wodehouse's work, and was angered by his enormous popularity. The reference to childishness is at the heart of the matter. Personally Orwell had come to Wodehouse as a delighted schoolboy, and knew in a literal sense just how great his childish appeal was.[34] Others of a certain age had had the same experience – they had started out as enthusiastic readers of his school stories. However, the point that needs emphasis is more ambitious than this. There was, if not a sustained childishness, then a sustained youthfulness in Wodehouse and it did have a very great appeal. His own values were those he received in his late Victorian Public School, and they never left him. Amongst other things he thoroughly admired athletic achievement, delighted in a rather playful kind of scholarship, valued good male friends highly and was invariably romantic in his view of women – even, deep down, when they were aunts. Wodehouse had no desire to shake off the attitude to work and leisure that he had imbibed along with Greek, Latin, cricket, rugby and boxing. Most work was a tiresome necessity for the great majority of mankind; the preferred state was one of leisured ease in which the pursuit of leisure in country houses, on golf courses, at the theatre and so on was central to day-to-day existence. He was overtly a chronicler of the leisured classes. As he knew himself, he was, above all, an Edwardian, and it was the leisured classes of that period that he wrote about – even when he was writing novels set in the 1970s.

P. G. Wodehouse was a case of arrested development; this did not bother him, and it has never bothered countless contented readers, and watchers and listeners too. Even his enthusiasm for cricket and rugby was concentrated on the doings of Dulwich teams. It was a bit odd, as he confided to Townend, but there it was. Dulwich had been like Heaven when he was there, and he was devoted to it for the rest of his life. When others were worrying about the great issues of the world, he was worrying about 'The Bedford Match'. As he wrote to Townend at the end of 1936, 'Incidentally, isn't it amazing that you and I, old buffers of fifty-five with civilisation shortly about to crash, can worry about school football? It is really the only thing I do worry about.'[35] This attitude, by no means an affectation, was to contribute to his remarkably stupid actions in Berlin, but it was also one that sustained his successful career. He could be pulled into what most people would see as reality, say when Billy Griffith was on the edge of securing a regular place in the England Test Team, but it did not happen often.[36] His very use of language had a permanent period ring to it, in his letters and ordinary speech, not just in his creative writing. He 'toddled', just as Bertie did.[37] Of course he was capable of creating the unpleasant Spode, later Lord Sidcup, something of a spoof Mosley, and we find a politically active female in *Aunts Aren't Gentlemen*, but Spode is a buffoon easily thwarted.[38] Wodehouse had a horror of creating what he thought of as 'real' characters. It was not his style. Wodehouse could certainly recognise the quality of 'realistic' writing, even when for a man with his background and values it was distasteful. He recognised that Mailer's *The Naked and the Dead* was very good.[39] For himself, like Jane Austen herself, he stuck to what he knew, and perfected his specialised art.[40] Agreeably enough his heroes and heroines usually combined romantic attachment with a certain kind of level-headedness on matters financial, again like Miss Austen's creations. Like hers, his work was peopled by those who await an inheritance, are dependent on the whim of a wealthy relative (often an aunt, uncle or guardian rather than a parent) or are otherwise waiting for something to turn up. They will not and should not have to work, save perhaps in a very acceptable profession. Essentially they cultivate the virtues of a leisured society. After all, to turn to Dickens, a more obviously direct influence on Wodehouse, even Mr Micawber became a proper gentleman, even though he had to go to Australia to do it. As far as we know, Ukridge never entirely did the trick, but then butlers, albeit ex-butlers, recognised him as an amateur and a gentleman. The remarkably hard-working Wodehouse spent his creative life among amateurs and gentlemen, and his popularity as a writer suggests that this fantastical world, like worlds created by successful science fiction writers, appealed to some deeply held prejudices and preferences among his readers.

Notes

1. R. Usborne, *Wodehouse at Work to the End* (Harmondsworth, 1976) p. 14. Usborne makes the point against himself.

2. On footnotes, see the Foreword Wodehouse wrote to *Over Seventy*. Along with *Bring on the Girls* and *Performing Flea*, *Over Seventy* has been collected to form *Wodehouse on Wodehouse* (London, 1980). Penguin produced the book in 1981. The author's send-up of footnotes can be found, pp. 468–471, in this edition. I will try to keep mine to the minimum.

3. Hilaire Belloc develops a well known elaboration on just how good Wodehouse was in his Introduction to *Week-End Wodehouse* (London, 1940) pp. v–x.

4. See Wodehouse's own Preface to the 1974 Penguin edition of *Sam the Sudden*, pp. 9–10.

5. Amid the welter of writing and television and radio programmes on this issue, I still think Orwell had some sensible things to say, as did Muggeridge, Compton Mackenzie . . . For a perhaps too vigorous a defence of Wodehouse see chapter 7 of Benny Green, *P. G. Wodehouse: A Literary Biography* (London, 1981). Orwell on Wodehouse can be found in *The Collected Essays of George Orwell* (London, 1961), Compton Mackenzie in *My Life and Times* (London, 1969), Muggeridge in T. Cazalet-Keir (ed.), *Homage to P. G. Wodehouse* (London, 1973). This footnote could go on.

6. In 1968 Wodehouse went to the extent of asking *Do Butlers Burgle Banks?* (London, 1968).

7. *Wodehouse on Wodehouse* (Harmondsworth, 1981) p. 477.

8. To enter the great debate, my favourite novel is *The Code of the Woosters* (London, 1938).

9. *Jeeves takes Charge* in *Jeeves Omnibus* (London, 1931) p. 14.

10. Mike Jackson appears in a number of Wodehouse school stories, notably *Mike* (London, 1909). He makes his exit in *Leave it to Psmith* (London, 1923).

11. The latter cited above, the former in *Psmith in the City* (London, 1910).

12. Benny Green makes this point in *P. G. Wodehouse: A Literary Biography* (London, 1981) chapter 2.

13. *Heavy Weather* (Harmondsworth, 1966) p. 40.

14. Ibid., p. 10.

15. R. Usborne, op. cit., p. 119.

16. The major collection of Ukridge stories is *Ukridge* (London, 1924).

17. *Mulliner Omnibus* (London, 1935) p. 765.

18. See, for instance, the collection *The Heart of a Goof* (London, 1926).

19. *Bachelors Anonymous* (Harmondsworth, 1975) p. 24.

20. *Summer Moonshine* (London, 1938) actually includes an unqualified monster, a woman, the Princess von und zu Dwornitzchek.

21. *Sam the Sudden* (Harmondsworth, 1974) p. 11.

22. Ibid., p. 14.

23. See, passim, *Performing Flea* in *Wodehouse on Wodehouse*.

24. Wodehouse was happy to laugh at the worst excesses of the school spirit, even in his early school stories, including those published in *The Captain*.

25. See F. Donaldson *P. G. Wodehouse: A Biography* (London, 1982). For a

striking example, note Ethel's determined work in Hollywood.

26. *Sam the Sudden* p. 222.
27. Ibid., p. 244.
28. Ibid., p. 238.
29. See, for example, *The Pothunters* (London, 1902).
30. See a letter to Townend in *Performing Flea* in *Wodehouse on Wodehouse*, p. 381. This letter also emphasises the centrality in Pelham's life of Dulwich's sporting success and Pekes.
31. Ibid., p. 378.
32. D. Krause (ed.), *The Letters of Sean O'Casey*, vol. I (London, 1975) p. 890.
33. Ibid., p. 882.
34. P. Stansky and W. Abrahams *The Unknown Orwell* (London, 1972).
35. *Wodehouse on Wodehouse*, p. 329.
36. Ibid., p. 363.
37. Richard Usborne sees more evidence of change. See op.cit. p. 202–3.
38. Early Spode can be found in *The Code of the Woosters* (London, 1938), later Spode in *Much Obliged, Jeeves* (London, 1971). There are other appearances. *Aunts Aren't Gentlemen* (London, 1974) was the last completed novel.
39. *Wodehouse on Wodehouse*, p. 393.
40. This goes for his work in the musical theatre, which I have not discussed. Much of Benny Green's book concentrates on the Wodehouse of the West End and, much more importantly, Broadway.

5

Leisure in Western Painting

Cyril Barrett

The thesis I wish to propose in this paper is that the depiction of leisure in Western painting coincides with the liberation of art itself as a full-time leisure activity.

I have confined myself to Western painting because I know a little about it. Whether the thesis would hold for Oriental, African or pre-Colombian painting I cannot say.

In trying to establish this thesis I have had to cover a wide area and do so seemingly superficially, but there is no other way. It is to be hoped that it can be tested by counter-examples, my own and others'.

Two preliminary remarks. First, what is meant by leisure? As I have argued elsewhere, almost any activity or occupation can, in some circumstances, be regarded as leisure. Yet, as I have argued in the same place, one can distinguish between leisure *per se* or presumptive, e.g. conversation, listening to music, feasting, sport, reading and suchlike activities, and leisure *per accidens*, e.g. interior decorating, brick-laying, farming, cooking, driving, market gardening and other activities usually regarded as tasks. Then there are borderline cases such as love-making and self-decorating and the occupations of painting or writing. My policy is to eschew the *per accidens* cases, take the *per se* cases for granted, and argue the borderline cases.

Secondly, I should like to point out that there are two approaches to the question of art and leisure. One is sociological; the other aesthetic. The sociological or socio-historical approach follows the history of leisure – the kinds of leisure activities pursued in different classes of society at different periods in history – as it is recorded pictorially. This is a fascinating line of inquiry which has been admirably pursued by such scholars as John Armitage. But, for the most part, the best evidence – marginal drawings in manuscripts, newspaper photographs – are not of a very high aesthetic quality. They illustrate leisure through the ages, just as do writings of whatever kind, whether letters, newspaper reports, advertisements or private journals. But, as the latter are not generally regarded as literature (except in the sense in which a government handout is), so these illustrations, for the most part, cannot be regarded as art. Now, it is with the depiction of leisure as art, or rather as having an aesthetic quality somewhat more than its informative interest, that I am concerned. And this generates a problem.

Although leisure has been a theme *in* art almost from the beginning, it has been a theme *of* art only within the last hundred years or so. To be sure, leisure subjects such as listening to or playing music, feasting, sport and such like have been themes of art. But initially they were not depicted for their own sake, rather for some ulterior purpose. What these purposes were I shall discuss in the course of the paper. The point I wish to make here, and the problem with which I am concerned, is that initially leisure was not regarded as a serious enough subject-matter for art. How it came to be taken seriously – though not, it is to be stressed, given disproportionate importance – throws light on the development of Western art.

It is reasonable to assume that painting initially had an exclusively utilitarian role, primarily ritual, commemorative or admonitory. It is more likely that cave paintings had a magical significance than that they were the equivalent of hunting prints or, as Chesterton suggests, nursery decorations: prehistoric prototypes of Billy the Bison or Harry the Horse. But there are also depictions of leisure activities, particularly of dancing and the use of musical instruments.

The Egyptians were most meticulous in depicting the agricultural and horticultural activities of the afterlife since, for them, life continued after death much as it had done in this life. There is much feasting, bearing of gifts, dancing and music to entertain the Pharaohs, nobles and important individuals. In this the Egyptians were unique. Whereas other races and cultures depicted great events and great personages or their gods, they rarely, if ever, depicted domestic events or leisure activities. It is highly unlikely that the Egyptians would have depicted what, for the ancients, must have been regarded as trivia, were it not for their peculiar notion of the afterlife.

Unfortunately little remains of Greek painting, and its statuary and reliefs are mainly devoted to serious subjects: gods, heroes and heroic events. However, from the Roman and Etruscan paintings that have survived in Pompeii, Herculaneum and the Necropolis of Tarquinia in Tuscany, and from Greek vases, we have a fairly wide record of leisure activities: feasting, dancing, acting, playing musical instruments, love-making, and what can reasonably be construed as conversation and debate. This is the visual equivalent of the Greco-Roman attitude towards leisure as described in literature – in Homer, Horace, Pliny, Sappho, Catullus, Plato, and Aristotle.

We have moved a stage further, whether backwards or forwards, from the Egyptians. Enjoyment of leisure is seen as a desirable goal in this life and not solely in the afterlife. Not that the Egyptians would have shunned or despised the enjoyment of leisure in this life. But for them this life was too transitory. Real and everlasting ('eternal') life began after death. For the Greco-Romans the afterlife was problematical. If there was to be leisure it must be here and now. *Carpe diem.*

Then came Christianity. It was not that the Christians had no time for leisure; they had a little or no graphic time for it. Like the Egyptians their sights were set on a future life. Unlike the Egyptians, however, the afterlife was not to be a replica of the pleasures of this present life. At most it was an allegory based on the present life. The prime analogue was the garden. This could be the Garden of Eden, or the enclosed mystical garden. Curiously enough, among Muslim cultures, to which animal representational art was forbidden, the Persians also used the allegory of the Garden of Paradise as the symbol of heavenly bliss.

But, for the most part, Christian painting and sculpture had little or nothing to do with leisure in this life before the Avignon popes of the fourteenth century. Then, for the first time in a thousand years, the pleasures of leisure were depicted. Whether or not these scenes of plants, animals and people at their ease strictly depict leisure activities, they certainly reflect the increased interest in depicting what would hitherto have been regarded as secular subjects too trivial to be recorded. These pictures show a gradual trend towards a form of art that was not confined to religious, political or historical subjects. The process towards secularisation was very gradual. However, by the fifteenth century leisure scenes such as hunting appear in illustrations, e.g. Books of Hours. (In the Middle Ages hunting was virtually the only leisure activity, and that the privilege of the rich.)

Yet for centuries the most one finds in the depiction of leisure are mythological or allegorical scenes of gods roistering or engaged in amours. The revival of pagan classical mythology in the fourteenth century, and progressing into the fifteenth and sixteenth centuries, gave artists an opportunity to depict leisure. But here we must be careful. Although eating at table is commonly regarded as a leisure activity, it is hardly appropriate to regard pictures of the Last Supper, the Miracle of the Loaves and Fishes or the Marriage Feast of Cana as depictions of leisure activities. Likewise Giovanni Bellini's *The Feast of the Gods* (1514), a picnic scene painted for the Duke of Ferrara, though, perhaps, on a slightly or distinctly lower spiritual level, is not exactly a depiction of an ordinary alfresco binge. Botticelli's *Primavera* (1477) poses a different kind of problem. There is leisure activity, to wit, dancing and music, but it is not only celebrating the simple joys of spring. It incorporates mysterious, neo-Platonic ideas, not incompatible with a homely notion of leisure but decidedly something more. Yet there was the occasional straightforward, if somewhat stylised, leisure scene, such as *The Hunt* by Uccello (1396–7). For him a hunt was perhaps no more a leisure event than a battle was a serious encounter.

Thus things continued well into the sixteenth century. Serious Renaissance painters, such as Michelangelo, Leonardo, Raphael and Dürer, to say nothing of sculptors, continued to paint, sculpt and draw serious religious, political, historical or scientific subjects. However, some were coming to treat art as perhaps it had always been treated, at least by some artists, as, itself, a leisure activity. They painted self-portraits, portraits of unknown ladies and gentlemen, flowers, landscapes and even the occasional still-life – a basket of fruit or game and vegetables piled on a kitchen table. This was art for art's sake, not art in the service of state or church or of a rich patron. It was art for the artist's sake: pure recreation: pure self-indulgence, though hard work.

Towards the end of the sixteenth century art flourished in Venice and Burgundy, which embraced the Netherlands. Both of these regions were extremely prosperous, not, it must be said, in industry and manufacture, but in trade, which in its way is not a dishonourable pursuit. Venice produced Titian, Giorgione, Tintoretto and Veronese. Of these I find Titian the most interesting from the point of view of the depiction of leisure. He, so to speak, bridges the gap between those painters who depicted leisure in its true form and those who depicted it in its mythological disguise. His *Bacchanalia* (1520) is a binge disguised in mythological form. *Bacchus and Ariadne* (1522) is the tailend of a binge with an element of courtship, surely a civilised leisure activity. More interesting is the gorgeous *Diana and Actaeon* (1559) showing Diana and her maids bathing in the nude, the only proper way to do it. Finally, there is a theme that reappears through the ages, a toilet scene. *The Toilet of Venus* (1565) may be its ancestor. Washing and dressing are not in themselves leisure activities, but they may be conducted in a leisurely manner and give titillation to aged voyeurs.

One could argue that Tintoretto's delightful *Susanna and the Elders* (1551) was a leisure picture with voyeurs since, like Diana and her attendants (and, presumably, Venetian ladies generally), she was enjoying a cooling dip in the nude. With Veronese, however, the depiction of leisure takes a more positive turn. His *Feast in the House of Levi/Last Supper* (1562) and his other pictures of biblical carousing were nothing less than somewhat exaggerated (one suspects) celebrations of some of the more sumptuous Venetian banquets of the time, for which he was gently but firmly reprimanded by the Inquisition. Yet it was Titian's almost exact contemporary, Giorgione, who produced what may be construed as leisure pictures, the enigmatic *The Tempest* (1508) and the equally equivocal *Rustic Concert* (1509).

Outside Italy, particularly in the Empire, which in the sixteenth century, by many matrimonial fiddles, included not only Germany but also Spain (under Charles V), what had once been Burgundy and what is now Belgium and Holland, the depiction of leisure activities, mostly of low life, became popular. Paradoxically the Spanish, while not failing to be aristocratic, were also populist, and the Netherlanders even more so. Thus you have Velazquez painting emperors and kings disporting themselves (*Philip IV on a boar hunt* (1645)) and also ordinary folk having a good, if rowdy, time (*The Merrymakers* (1628), *Topers* (1629)). I am not sure that *Las Meninas* (1656) with the Infanta, maids, dog, observing parents and court painter cannot be regarded as a leisure picture of domestic fun, tranquillity and happiness, but I shall not press this.

However, it was in the Low Countries that leisure activities became a major subject for painting. And it was mainly, though not exclusively, of a rumbustious, peasant kind. Pieter Brueghel, the Elder, was the chief exponent of this genre. His *Children at Play*

(1560) and hearty *Wedding Dance* (1566) have come down as typical of the genre; but I think his *Hunters* (1565), showing two huntsmen on a hill in snow looking down on skaters on a frozen pond below, among the finest leisure pictures ever painted, though others regard it as a contrast between work and leisure.

Brueghel was followed in the seventeenth century by Frans Hals, Rubens, Steen, even Vermeer and Ruisdael and many others. Hals, though he painted many *bon viveurs*, such as, presumably, *The Laughing Cavalier*, rarely painted them in action. *The Banquet of the Civic Guard of the Archers of St George* is as unvivacious as any set group portrait by Rembrandt. Rubens, on the other hand, though a man of strict observance, despite his fondness for fleshed women, celebrated such leisure activities as a lion hunt (1617), a kermesse (1631) and his *The Garden of Love* (1632). (His famous *Le chapeau de paille* (1622), as all paintings depicting high fashion, along with depictions of an elegant toilet, may be regarded as a leisure picture rather than simply the portrait of an attractive woman.) Dutch and Flemish artists – Jan Steen, Frans Snyders, and Ruisdael – devoted themselves to hunting scenes, tavern scenes and food: game, vegetables and fruit mostly. These latter pictures, it is said, were designed to stimulate appetites at mealtimes.

But the artist of the period who captured the spirit of leisure most perfectly was Vermeer. He was out of his time in that he was already painting for painting's sake. He was also outside his time in another sense: he captured the timeless tranquillity of leisure, whether it be a girl seated at a virginal or standing at one or playing a guitar or simply reading a letter – for letter-writing must be, after contemplation and conversation, one of the most civilised of leisure activities.

The eighteenth century saw a further incursion into the world of leisure, particularly in France, but also in Italy and, to a lesser extent, the United Kingdom and Spain. In France the painters of leisure were pre-eminently Watteau, Boucher, Fragonard, Lancret and Pater. Their depiction of *fêtes galantes*, dancing, theatricals, buffoonery, love-making, hunting and food were not incidental to their oeuvre, as with earlier painters, but its central preoccupation. In this they reflected the effete age of Louis XV (1715–74) and Louis XVI (1774–93), the age of rococo triviality. Louis XIV, in order to control the nobles, had brought them to Paris where they attended at court and had little political power. They whiled away their time in such leisure pursuits as the artists depicted.

The English aristocracy were more robust. That they engaged in leisure pursuits more than previously is probable. Apart from the Jacobite rebellions of '15 and '45 there was little internal strife in Britain, so they had leisure time. This seems to have been mostly spent in hunting, horse-racing, fishing, bull and bear-bating, cock-fighting, playing a primitive form of cricket or golf, gambling, card playing, and, of course, eating and drinking and having conversations in taverns and coffee-houses. Some of these activities were recorded by Hogarth, Stubbs, Zoffany and the sporting artists. Hogarth's *The Rake's Progress* (1735) and his *Marriage à la mode* (1743) depict the more sordid and bizarre aspects of English eighteenth-century life, high and low, as does Hogarth's *Beer St* (1751). In this respect English artists seem to hold a balance between the almost exclusively aristocratic French and the demotic painters of the Low Countries. The theatre has a prominent place in English, as in French, art of the period. It was the age of Garrick and Mrs Siddons. Hogarth and Zoffany painted them but, in general, the quality of theatrical painting in England at the time was rather low, as a visit to the Garrick Club will confirm. Sporting paintings and, especially, prints were becoming popular at this time. Ironically the only work of any quality was that of Stubbs, who was more interested in the anatomies of animals than in their performances on the race course or elsewhere. For all that, he did the racing fraternity proud, one way or another. Zoffany suggested rather than depicted convivial social life in his rather formal group portraits in a domestic setting. Hogarth did it somewhat less formally.

Goya's early pictures (cartoons for tapestries), like Velazquez's early work, were of peasants enjoying themselves. Tiepolo, Guardi and Longhi, in Italy, also indulged in recording the frivolities of their native Venice. To Longhi we are indebted for an early depiction of a popular leisure activity, looking at other animals, in this case a rhinoceros.

At about this time (the late eighteenth century) a rift in the visual arts was beginning to occur which became manifest in the mid-nineteenth century and is reflected in the depiction of leisure. It is between academic, as against free, art, or what later came to be called 'avant-garde' art. The academics, by and large, tended to paint serious religious, historical or classical subjects and important portraits. This was true of all of them, particularly in the nineteenth century, but of none more so than those of the Royal Academy, London, founded in 1768 and dominated by Reynolds, who favoured a lofty style in the 'grand manner'. Academicians eschewed rococo frivolity.

To suggest, however, that the eighteenth century saw the rift between the academic and an art that was less pompous and conservative, more experimental and adventurous, that would develop in the nineteenth century, would be most misleading. Hogarth, who was connected with the two St Martin's Lane academies, forerunners of the Royal Academy, produced work that belonged in both camps. Besides painting low and fashionable life he also painted in the 'grand manner' for example *The Pool of Bethesda* and *The Good Samaritan* (1735–6). Gainsborough was an academician and yet his techniques of painting portraits and landscapes were poles apart from those of Reynolds. These pictures raise once again the question of whether they are leisure pictures or whether what they are depicting can be regarded as related to leisure. It can be said that interest in Nature and landscape had become a leisure activity, as had the study of birds, animals and plants. As for fashionable portraits such as those painted by Gainsborough and Romney, these, as has been said, are not unconnected with leisure.

In France, about this time, academicism was even more classical; serious and austere in the hands of David, Ingres and the neoclassicists. Though, as dictator of the arts during the French Revolution, David abolished the Academy, he helped to substitute another kind of academy, the Institute. He repudiated the rococo early in his career, adopted neoclassicism and devoted himself to classical, moral, historical and patriotic subjects. There was no room in his work for the depiction of leisure. Ingres was less austere, using as he did a sinuous line. Some of his nudes are positively voluptuous, and are occasionally depicted bathing, particularly in seraglios. Whether these pictures should be regarded as leisure pictures or merely settings for nudes is hard to say; if the former, they are rare in Ingres' œuvre.

If Ingres is an exception to my thesis that leisure subjects tend to be favoured by less conventional, freer and more experimental artists, the Romantics question it even more strongly. Though both Géricault and his admirer Delacroix broke with classical subjects and academic techniques, they rarely made use of leisure subjects, apart from horse-racing (Géricault) or lion hunting (Delacroix). They were concerned with contemporary events – *The Raft of the Medusa*, *The Massacre of Chios*, *Liberty at the Barricades* – or the plight of the poor and mad, the works of Shakespeare and Walter Scott, oriental exotica and such like. Géricault's output was too small – he died at the age of thirty-three. Delacroix's position was ambiguous. In popular belief, and indeed among certain sections of received wisdom, Delacroix was *the* Romantic, Ingres, *the* classical painter of the time. A Romantic painter Delacroix may have been, but he was also a painter in the classical tradition. One very remarkable thing about Delacroix, particularly in his later years, was the ease and freedom of his first sketches, compared with the deathly dullness of the finished, 'worked up' picture. (Constable also suffered in this respect from the influence of academicism, the finished, well-constructed work.) The truth is that, though seeming polar opposites, romanticism and classicism, in France as in England and elsewhere, were divided by a very vague distinction.

It is not until we come to Manet that we find the rejection of academicism (in the person of Couture) coupled with an interest in leisure subjects, and an artist with a new and exciting style that aroused the admiration of his generation, which included the Impressionists, (Degas, Cézanne and Renoir). His earlier pictures centred around a group of Spanish dancers who had come to Paris – *The Guitarist* (1860), *Lola de Valence* (1862), bullfights (though he did not visit Spain until 1865) – and other scenes of leisure, including the ambitious *Concert in the Tuileries Gardens* (1860) which has recently been sold to Japan for a King's ransom. 1863 witnessed a leisure picture that caused some notoriety at the Salon des Refusés: *Déjeuner sur l'herbe* (literally 'Lunch on the Grass', but, more discreetly, 'Bathing Picnic'). The fact that the figures, updated, came from Raphael's *The Judgement of Paris* via an engraving by that insignificant Florentine, Marc Antonio, did little to assuage public indignation. Manet went on to paint scenes in bars (*Le Bon Bock*, 1873), scenes in theatres (*The Bar of the Folies-Bergères*, 1882), boating scenes, scenes at the races and other leisure pursuits. A picture (1870) of Eva Gonzalès painting could be included among them, though possibly not the notorious *Olympia* (1865) for, though her profession was related to leisure, the picture is that of a recumbent nude in the classical manner with some modern accessories.

It has been said of Manet that he was an academician *manqué* and that, had that fraternity been prepared to accept him, he could have rejuvenated it by his fresh and adventurous use of the Old Masters. Be that as it may, one can be in no doubt about the

Impressionists whom he influenced and who influenced him, some say for the worse. They made a clear break; if not with the past, at least with the current interpretation of it by the academicians. For them painting itself had become fully a leisure activity to be pursued for its own sake and not to please a patron, to arouse religious devotion or morally elevate or satirise or politically stimulate or for any of those extra-pictorial purposes to which it had been traditionally devoted. This is not to say that it was artistically the better for this liberation and autonomy. Nor does it mean that this was how the hard core of Impressionists – Monet, Sisley and Pissarro – viewed what they were doing. They believed that they were presenting the world, literally, in its true light, as it is seen. Those on the fringes of Impressionism, Whistler in particular, knew better. They saw it for what it was: art for art's sake.

Unlike Manet, it has to be confessed, the Impressionists rarely took leisure activities, apart from boating on a river, as their subject matter. Mostly they painted landscapes, in all weathers and at different times of day. Monet concentrated on poplars, haystacks, Rouen Cathedral, London – in particular the Thames – and the waterlilies in the pond in his garden at Giverny. Apart from boating and bathing, gardening and gardens were the principal leisure subjects the Impressionists depicted. This may have been no accident since the garden, great (i.e. landscape-garden) or small, is a kind of picture. Indeed, if it is allowed that in an earlier age landscape painting was, indirectly, a reflection of leisure activity, the concentration of the Impressionists on both gardens and landscape argues that they were totally immersed in leisure, both in their attitude to the artist's role and in their subject matter.

If this is true, then it is most revealing. It tells us something about the Impressionists and those artists closely associated with them, such as Degas, Renoir, Cézanne, Seurat and Toulouse-Lautrec; and it tells us it in terms of the depiction of leisure. For, unlike the Impressionists, these other painters depicted leisure subjects as such, and not merely as props for exploring colour and light. The subjects were mostly those with which we are by now familiar: landscapes or walking in the country, gardens or people sitting in them, picnics, bathing, and other healthy outdoor pursuits including horse-racing, boating and sailing, and such games as tennis; and indoor pursuits such as drinking in bars and cafés, theatre and cabaret, dancing and the circus, dalliance and enticement thereto. These subjects have inspired masterpieces.

Subsequent artists, the Post-Impressionist, Fauve, Cubist, Da-
daist and Orphic Cubist (Delaunay), not to mention later manifes-
tations, such as Pop Art, in one way or another – and these ways
are often distinctly odd – depict or embody leisure activities. I shall
not follow them, because the point has now been reached when I
can leave the history of Western painting. What follows is more of
the same. But before drawing conclusions I should like to make a
few immediate points.

First, it should be understood that, while Manet, Degas, Renoir,
Lautrec, Seurat and the Impressionists painted what might be
called leisure subjects and painted them as such, this was only a
part of their œuvre, even if a major part. It was a part of the wider
movement towards 'ordinary' rather than classical subjects. Thus,
along with picnickers and concert goers, Manet painted absinthe
drinkers and roadmenders. Besides ballerinas, Degas painted ordinary folk washing. Renoir painted such activities as tying a shoe-
lace; and Lautrec took the world around him in Montmartre almost
as it came: cabaret artists, prostitutes, clowns and dropouts. Of
those I have mentioned, only the Impressionists and Seurat did
not show the seamy side of life. But even they were not devoted to
depicting leisure. Their main concern was with their art. Subject
matter was incidental. Bathing and boating, gardens and landscapes, served their purposes admirably, since none involved
vigorous action nor had they any significance beyond themselves.
These artists, however, if not the depictors of leisure, were the
exemplifications of leisure *par excellence*; they painted for, and
solely for, painting's sake.

But the main thesis of this paper is that the conditions for
depicting leisure as a subject in its own right are: (a) the acceptance
of scenes from ordinary life as fit subjects for painting; and (b) an
indulgence in painting for its own sake where triviality of subject
matter is of little or no adverse importance.

As we have seen, leisure activities have been depicted throughout the ages, but mainly for ulterior purposes or under various
disguises – entertainment in the afterlife; the roistering and
amours of the gods; to add local colour to a royal portrait; or as a
record of popular, often derisory, occupations. It is significant that
the pockets of admirable depictions of leisure – the Low Countries
and Spain (Brueghel, Velazquez, Hals, Vermeer) and the French
court of the eighteenth century (Watteau, Fragonard, Boucher) –
were made possible either by genuine demotic and democratic

feelings or by a blatant disregard of accepted standards of taste, coupled with a feeling for painting as a desirable end in itself and not as a means towards moral, religious, political or other ends.

But it was Manet, the Impressionists and the Post-Impressionists who finally established the depiction of leisure subjects, if not as the sole subjects worth depicting, at least as worthy subjects, subjects capable of generating great works of art such as *Déjeuner sur l'herbe* and *The Bar of the Folies-Bergères* by Manet; Renoir's *Moulin de la Galette* and *The Boating Party*; or Seurat's *Bathers at Asnières*, *Sunday on the Island of La Grande Jatte* and *The Circus*. At the same time they established painting itself as a worthwhile activity in its own right irrespective of what worthy (or unworthy) purposes it might serve. They re-established it as an expression of free human spirit. In this they were at one with the Greeks, though whether the Greeks would have recognised them we cannot say. My suspicion is that they would have done so.

6

Audiences, Art and Theatre: The Justification of Leisure and Images of the Eighteenth-Century English Stage

Shearer West

In 1749 the anonymous *Essay on Tragedy* tackled the critical analysis of Samuel Johnson's turgid *Irene*. Its starting point was a justification of theatrical entertainment which involved a condemnation of other forms of leisure activity. The author censured entertainments such as Vauxhall, a pleasure garden formed for lazy enjoyment, eating, listening to music and occasionally engaging in clandestine copulation amongst the garden's numerous hedgerows. Even more within the anonymous critic's line of fire was card playing – not only a waste of time but, through its inevitable concomitant, gambling, a possible incentive to corruption. To the author of the *Essay on Tragedy*, the only truly justifiable form of leisure entertainment was the theatre, which, he claimed, 'stimulate[s] us to the practice of every virtue that can dignify and adorn our natures'.[1]

The generally corrupt nature of many fashionable and unfashionable London pastimes was hard to deny. Foreign visitors commented with disgust on the senseless cruelty of cock fighting, and the activities of such groups as the Hellfire Club suggested the extremes to which men of leisure could go to fill their empty hours. Hogarth pointed to such corruption in *The Rake's Progress* (1731–5), in which the profligate Tom Rakewell, reacting against his late father's miserliness, fritters away his newly acquired fortune on dancing lessons, racehorses and classically landscaped gardens, filling his remaining leisure hours with drunken sensuality. Such idle gentlemen had less force in a flourishing and energetic society and, as early as 1715, Jonathan Richardson found it necessary to justify the practice of art-collecting as a means of keeping the idle rich off the streets:

> Men of easy and plentiful fortunes have commonly a great part of their time at their own disposal, and the want of knowing how to pass these hours away, in virtuous amusements, contributes perhaps as much to the mischievous effects of vice, as covetousness, pride, lust, love of crime, or any passion whatsoever.[2]

Leisure, according to Richardson, should be 'profitably employed'.

A more apparent tempering influence came in the form of the theatre – defended by numerous eighteenth-century writers, although attacked by a seemingly ubiquitous stream of clergymen from the beginning of the eighteenth century to the end of it. The undeniable popularity of the theatre in the eighteenth century was due, in no small part, to the Licensing Act of 1737 – the government imposition of censorship onto the stage. Not only did every new play have to find its way past the strict eye of the Lord Chamberlain, but only three theatres were allowed to present plays in London: Drury Lane and Covent Garden in the winter, and the Haymarket in the summer. Historians of the eighteenth-century theatre are inevitably evasive about the exact composition of the theatre audience, as the available statistics are unhelpful. Theatre-going was certainly an upper-class pastime, but the evidence suggests that it was also beginning to be accessible to a larger public.[3] Hogarth's print, *The Laughing Audience* (1733) contrasts these 'vulgar' but monied merchant classes, who laugh openly at the performance, with the fops in the gallery who are more interested in posing and cavorting with the orange-sellers. Hogarth finds the humour of the fashionable but oblivious audience again in one version of *The Beggar's Opera* (Plate 1), where members of the nobility – then allowed the privilege of sitting on the stage – appear to be less than interested in the play itself. The most ardent observer, the Duke of Bolton, on the right, was at the time having an affair with Lavinia Fenton, the actress playing Polly Peachum – hence his excessive, and indeed socially unnecessary, interest in the action of the play. The 1750 *Guide to the Stage* sums up the unwritten rules of this gentrified audience most ironically. It exhorts:

Never laugh at what passes on stage save it be an error, blunder, or accident. In tragic scenes avoid being visibly moved by humming a tune, regarding the audience, engaging in conversation, or turning your back to the stage. When a female social rival calls attention to herself and away from the stage, let fall your handkerchief into the pit, or call out to an acquaintance in the opposite box, or burst into loud and unexpected laughter.[4]

How can this view of a bored and socially self-conscious audience be reconciled with Edmund Burke's rating: 'of the various means which idleness will take for its amusement, in truth I believe the theatre is the most innocent'? A consideration of this justification of the theatre will reveal how the audience, the supposed passive receptor of the moral lessons of the theatre, had in reality a very different and more complex relationship with the stage. In considering this dichotomy between representation and reality, it is necessary to refer both to writing about the stage, and to how the stage was represented in art. During the period in which the Licensing Act was enforced most severely (c. 1750–1817), a focus of attention was imposed upon London audiences, and their response to this was both various and revealing. The questions of the moral purpose of the theatre, the status of actors, and theatrical riots each elucidate how such a leisure activity was perceived in the eighteenth century.

Jeremy Collier's attack, in 1698, on the immorality and profaneness of the English stage was the first in a long line of dissension against stage representation. The homiletic fire-and-brimstone tone of most of these attacks involved such assertions as that of the anonymous author of *The Stage, the Highroad to Hell* (1767):

All arts are proofs of the degeneracy of the human species; for if man had not, by the fall, and its fatal consequences, forfeited his first exalted condition, he would never have occasion for invention to supply his wants, or education to remedy the imbecility of his nature.[5]

Theatrical entertainments were blamed for 'the downfall of kingdoms'; disasters in the theatre were attributed to divine retribution; the stage arts were equated with Popery, and women's virtue was seen to be threatened: '*Musick* softens,' warned one polemic, 'Company naturally awakes the Passions, the Sculpture,

Imagery, and Painting of the Building, help to alarm.'[6] Some early writers were reacting directly to the licentiousness of Charles II's court and the accompanying liberality of Restoration playwrights, to whom human vices were the stuff of which good comedy was made. However, these attacks persisted long after Restoration plays had been cleaned up and the Lord Chamberlain awarded the axe of censorship. Even after Garrick had made the stage an unquestionably acceptable form of entertainment, William Law's *The Absolute Unlawfulness of the Stage Entertainment Fully Demonstrated* (1726) went into its fourth edition and Samuel Foote's satire on Methodism, *The Minor* (1760) provoked a sustained pamphlet war.

However, even the more enlightened and liberal-minded writers did not simply praise the theatre without reservation. What they condemned in it was not its lack of spirituality, but rather its avoidance of sound civic values in favour of spectacle and display. Hogarth's *Masquerades and Operas* (Plate 2) was one of the few prints of the century to make this condemnation clear. A man is wheeling a cart full of 'waste paper' which, upon a closer examination, turns out to be the plays of Shakespeare, Dryden, and Congreve. The crowds are ignoring the loss of such noble work, because they are too busy queuing up for masquerades, operas and pantomimes, which will provide them with excitement, noise and spectacle, but very little stimulus for thought or edification. Pantomine spectacles were particularly popular throughout the eighteenth century, as they contained visual variety, rapid scene shifts and stage trickery. Such spectacles were the ammunition for humanist writers to attack the stage – laying the blame not on the playwrights but on the corrupt taste of the public. To observers such as Hogarth, bad taste was a reflection of deeper evils of society; the lack of sound moral judgement was reflected in a lack of artistic discernment.

The same writers who condemned pantomime claimed that more legitimate theatrical entertainments were a positive, educative force. Such plays as those of Shakespeare were not only meant to be seen, but they were also to be perused 'in the closet', where the full force of their moral instruction would become apparent. Artists also responded to this contrast between mindless pantomine and enriching tragedy. Hogarth's attack on *Masquerades and Operas* should be compared with his view of *David Garrick in the Character of Richard III* (Plate 3). Here Hogarth represents Garrick as

William Hogarth: *The Begger's Opera*, Version 6, oil on canvas, 1731, London.

William Hogarth: *Masquerades and Operas*, engraving, 1724, London.

3. William Hogarth: *Garrick as Richard III*, oil on canvas, 1745, Liverpool.

4. Sir Joshua Reynolds: *Mrs Siddons as the Tragic Muse*, oil on canvas, 1789, London.

5. George Carter: *The Apotheosis of David Garrick*, oil on canvas, 1782, Stratford-upon-Avon.

Sir Thomas Lawrence: *Kemble as Coriolanus*, oil on canvas, 1798, London.

7. (left) 'The Theatrical Ranter' engraving in *Carlton House Magazine*, 1794, London.

8. (right) James Gillray: *Pizarro Contemplating Over the Product of His New Peruvian Mine (Sheridan as Pizarro)*, coloured engraving, 1799, London.

9. Robert Dighton: *We Serve a King Whom We Love-A God Whom We Adore (Kemble as Rolla)*, etching, 1799.

10. Thomas Rowlandson: *Pigeon Hole: A Covent Garden Contrivance to Coop up the Gods*, coloured engraving, 1811, London.

the tragic Richard awakening from his dream, and the size of the picture, as well as the facial expression of Garrick, both suggest that Hogarth was attempting not just a portrait of Garrick but a history painting.[7] The obvious quotation from *The Tent of Darius* (1661) by the French academician Charles Le Brun would seem to justify such an interpretation of this work: Hogarth's scene was a realisation of a significant theatrical, and even historical, moment. Influential English writers, such as Richardson, borrowed from the French Academicians the idea that history painting – the represen- tation of heroic scenes from the Bible, literature and mythology – was the highest form of art. By showing Garrick as he did, Hogarth is suggesting that the theatrical art was worthy of such an elevated representation. Significantly, portraits of actors in character, often tragic character, were more common in the eighteenth century than views of pantomimes, despite the enormous popularity of the latter. Artists chose to represent Garrick in Shakespearian charac- ters, because Shakespeare was beginning to be seen as England's greatest dramatist, despite the continual stage representation of neoclassical 'revisions' of his work. Aside from the edification derived from plays such as those of Shakespeare, the discerning audience was to be edified further through the judgement and sensibility of such actors and actresses as Garrick, Siddons and Kemble. The detail with which an audience was meant to examine the performance of an actor can be seen by referring to any number of press criticisms in the eighteenth century. For example, a critic in the *Monthly Mirror* in 1795 described Kemble's performance in the last scene of *Alexander the Great* as follows:

> The expiring tone with which Kemble pronounces 'Cover me', his shivering, when wrapt round in the imperial robes; his wan and wasted countenance; the manner of his laboriously drawing his legs together, and their aguish knocking when they meet, surpass all description.[8]

Theatrical portraits were an extension of the idea that a play should be studied closely for its edifying message. Although such por- traits were sometimes commissioned by the actors themselves, more often than not the commission came from noblemen who added the paintings to their collections of portraits and Old Masters.[9]

Stage representation of tragedy was easier to justify on moral grounds than that of comedy, and there was, consequently, an undeniable difference between tragic and comic representation and justification in art and literature. Both forms of justification had recourse to classical literature, particularly Aristotle and Horace, so tragedy, like history painting, was to represent elevated characters. The critic William Cooke summed up the moral justification of tragedy most concisely in 1775, when he wrote:

> The advantage tragedy brings to mankind, is by no means inconsiderable: it prepares us to bear the most unlucky accidents courageously, and disposes the most miserable to think themselves happy, when they compare their own misfortunes with those which tragedy has represented to them . . . in exhibiting those *miserables* in what they suffer, it teaches us to stand our own guard, and powerfully induces us to moderate, and refine in ourselves what was the only cause of their loss.[10]

Zoffany's various portraits of actors in tragic roles reveal how such elevation functions in an artistic context. Zoffany presents the scene as it may have been performed, but such a convincing theatrical representation lacks the essential ingredient – the audience itself. We are thus not meant to see these works as pieces of documentation but as statements about tragedy and the actor's evocation of it.

Comic representation was more difficult to justify, and in its extreme forms could be subject to the moralist's admonitions against both spectacle and licence. But critics again referred to the ideas of Aristotle, as filtered through Horace and French neoclassicists such as René Rapin, to come up with a function for comedy which paralleled the purgation of pity and fear which was to be accomplished by tragedy. Philosophers tackled the problem of why people laugh: some, like Thomas Hobbes, extended the ancient notion that we laugh out of a sense of superiority – that comedy should render low and vulgar characters, as opposed to tragedy's elevated heroes. Others, such as Francis Hutcheson, put forth a more egalitarian view: we laugh when we sense an unlikely contrast or an incongruity. Laughing needed to be considered a good thing in order for comedy to be justified:

> Laughing is that noble faculty which distinguishes man from beast, which shows the rationality of the soul, that can be moved

independent of the sense; it is the mark of reason, the badge of good-humour, and the sign of mirth.[11]

Further arguments about the benefits of comedy came to the fore when the 'sentimental comedies' began dominating the London stage. These were seen by many as a self-congratulatory manifestation of idealistic bourgeois moralism, and many critics argued that straight comedy was more genuinely edifying: 'The soundest philosophers have agreed, that ridicule has a much better effect in curing the vices and imperfections of men, than the examples of rigid virtue.'[12] In theatrical portraiture, comedy was often treated with equal respect to tragedy, given the differences in their conventions and forms of representation. Zoffany's portrait of Garrick in the comic interlude, *The Farmer's Return* (1762; private collection) was compared by Horace Walpole to Dutch genre painting, and, given Zoffany's continental background, such an artistic equation could hardly have been an accident. Another portrait by Zoffany shows Mrs Abington as the Widow Bellmour in Arthur Murphy's comedy *The Way to Keep Him* (1764; Petworth), and here the famous comic actress is dignified by a setting which is not theatrical but is derived, in part, from one of the artist's portraits of the Royal Family (1764; Royal Collection). More often, representation of comic scenes was confined to caricature, which was seen as a more appropriate mode, as it conveyed aberrations of character, rather than perfections.

   Painting played an increasingly important role in the perpetuation of the idea that theatre was valuable and morally efficacious. When Reynolds became President of the Royal Academy in 1768 he proved that he was not averse to painting portraits of famous actors and actresses. He showed that, through these portraits, he could experiment freely with his theories of art, expounded in his Academy Discourses, particularly his assertion that portraiture could be elevated by borrowing qualities normally associated with history painting. His early theatrical portraits play with some of the conventions of the genre and serve to forge a new link between art and theatre. For example, *Mrs Abington as Miss Prue* puts her finger in her mouth: a pose adopted in some previous portraits of men, but considered too vulgar for female portraiture. Reynolds here uses the familiar pose in an unfamiliar context to underline the characterisation of the unrefined and wanton Miss Prue. His portrait of Garrick as Kitely in Jonson's *Every Man In His Humour*

(1768; Royal Collection) similarly relies on other conventions of portraiture: he dresses Garrick in a highly acceptable van Dyck collar and thus alludes to the age of Jonson himself, while studiously avoiding a more extravagant representation of Kitely's dominant humour, jealousy.

Reynolds carried his idea one step further in his portraits of *Garrick between Tragedy and Comedy* (1760–62; private collection) and *Mrs Siddons as the Tragic Muse* (Plate 4). The former shows a bewildered Garrick being pulled between the two Muses, and thus falls back on the iconography of the Judgement of Hercules, utilised by such history painters as Annibale Carracci and popularised in England by the Earl of Shaftesbury's *Characteristics* (1712). Here Garrick is no longer a performer but a hero with a dilemma, and Virtue and Vice have metamorphosed into Tragedy and Comedy. *Mrs Siddons as the Tragic Muse* likewise shows the actress as an abstraction, rather than as a specific character, and Reynolds has extended his learned allusions to Aristotle by including figures of Pity and Fear leaning over the actress's shoulder. The significance of this particular view of Siddons is underlined by the numerous anecdotes surrounding the work, including that of the actress herself, who claimed:

> When I attended him for the first sitting, after more gratifying encomiums than I can now repeat, he took me by the hand saying 'Ascend your undisputed throne and graciously bestow upon me some good idea of the Tragic Muse.' I walked up the steps and instantly seated myself in the attitude in which the Tragic Muse now appears.[13]

The pose was, in fact, borrowed from the figure of Isaiah on Michelangelo's Sistine ceiling. Such elevated representations bely contemporary popular prints of Siddons, such as the vitriolic *Melpomene* (1784), which shows the actress's tragic gesture employed for the less salubrious motive of acquiring more money.

By a natural extension, Reynolds's elevation of theatrical portraiture led to a more oblique use of actor portraits in history painting. John Boydell's ill-fated Shakespeare Gallery – intended to be a project to promote history painting – was invaded by the faces of Siddons and Kemble. For instance, James Northcote repainted his first version of the meeting of the princes in the tower from *Richard III* to include Kemble's unmistakable countenance, and Westall's painting of Lady Macbeth is really only a portrait of Siddons in one of her more famous roles.[14] Although these inclusions were, for the most part, unacknowledged, they would have been recognised and understood by the body of the public who regularly attended the theatre.

Further meanings accompanied the relationship between the character represented and the actor himself. Both Thomas Sheridan, the father of Richard Brinsley, and John Philip Kemble were known for their performances of Cato in Addison's play, and the famous scene in which Cato is contemplating suicide was represented in a similar way by both of them, despite their difference in generation. But the Cato of Sheridan was perceived by contemporary audiences as a noble declaimer of the ancient world, a symptom of the neoclassical mania which dominated British tragedy in the first half of the century. Kemble's Cato had more political implications, as Thomas Lawrence, who painted a portrait of Kemble as Cato, revealed. In a letter to his brother William, Lawrence stressed the nationalist sympathies that he felt Kemble's representation conjured up:

> I am convinced Mr Addison was ignorant [in] giving to the patriotism of Cato not the mere cold declamation of principle, but the rich enthusiasm of passion; and making him as much in love with his country, as Romeo is with his mistress.[15]

Cato had always been something of a politically controversial play, but here nuances of meaning were seen not only in the fictional role, but in the specific presentation of that role. The proponents of a moral justification for the theatre saw the actor as being a particularly important conveyor of this message. One observer wrote: 'The bulk of mankind have neither leisure nor faculties for very accurate study; they must be content with the interpretation of actors.'[16]

In order for the actor to be the intermediary in this audience/play relationship, it was necessary for a further literary and visual justification to be made. The poor reputation and low status of the actor before the eighteenth century would have made his or her role as moral mediator absurd. But in the rapidly changing eighteenth-century society, when class distinctions were becoming less rigidly defined, it is sometimes difficult to place the actor's social position. The stratification of society certainly no longer precluded actors from social climbing, but actors and actresses continued to be maligned for debauchery and prostitution. However, David Garrick realised the benefits of cultivating a more genteel reputation. He carried his mimic ability into his personal life and purchased a country estate, took the Grand Tour, entertained gentry and became an art patron.[17] Garrick's estate at Hampton was lavish and as modern as a country estate could be: the gardens were landscaped by Capability Brown, and the Adam brothers were involved in some of the architectural designs. Zoffany depicted Garrick on his estate in a series of conversation pieces, including one of Garrick and his wife standing in front of the so-called Shakespeare Temple, inside which was a statue of the Bard himself, executed by Roubiliac. While on the Grand Tour, Garrick also had his portrait painted in street dress by many fashionable painters in Italy at the time, including Pompeo Batoni who depicted him with his hand on a recent translation of Terence's comedies (1764; Oxford, Ashmolean). Although Garrick never considered producing Terence's comedies on his Drury Lane stage, this equation with a great classical comedian was intended to enhance the view the actor wished to project of himself.

When Garrick died, George Carter exhibited a large painting of him at the Royal Academy, called *The Apotheosis of David Garrick* (Plate 5). The work eulogises the actor in a way that would have been hitherto unacceptable, but it gets round the problem of glorifying a 'mere actor' by using a trick of academic history painting. Garrick's funeral cortège consists of other actors from Drury Lane but, rather than appearing at the funeral as themselves, these actors are presented in characteristic Shakespearian roles. By having Cordelia, Malvolio, Mrs Page and Hamlet appear at the funeral, rather than Miss Young, Mr Yates, Miss Pope and Mr Smith, Carter has implied that Garrick was not just an actor, but he was somehow the embodiment of the spirit of Shakespeare. To make the death of an actor the focus of allegory was highly unusual, and indeed would have been unheard of before, but, once Garrick had set a precedent for the gentrified actor, Kemble's biographers and apologists tried to outdo him.

Lawrence's iconic portraits of Kemble playing noble tragic characters such as Coriolanus (Plate 6) complemented the remarks made by some of Kemble's critics who insisted upon that actor's thorough grounding in the classics, genteel personal behaviour and high-class patronage:

He had inhaled from the pages of the ancient poets and historians, the lofty inspiration of Roman dignity; and indentifying
himself in imagination with the hero of Corioli, he abandoned
the consciousness of his actual self.[18]

This argument is fully in keeping with the insistence of dramatic
critics that actors should be well-grounded in the classics, grammar, oratory, history and fine arts. Furthermore, both Kemble's
biographer, James Boaden, and Garrick's biographer, Thomas
Davies, made cases for the gentlemanly habits cultivated by these
actors. Such insistence smacks of apologia, and the later writer,
Boaden, could not resist the implication that Kemble was the more
dignified and genteel of the two. 'Johnson objected to Garrick's
being admitted into his club,' Boaden gloats. 'He would not have
objected to Mr Kemble.'[19]

The obvious mythologising indulged in by such writers comes to
the fore in accounts of their heroes' childhoods. Thus Samuel
Foote, the greatest farce actor of the eighteenth century, has a very
different history from the noble tragedian Kemble. Their respective
biographers reveal that Kemble, when in school, effortlessly mem-
orised whole books of Homer, while Foote, the incipient comedian, was manufacturing artificial earthquakes to explode under
his master's desk.[20] The trickster was seen as somehow having a
different development from that of the tragedian. Kemble cultivated this image by performing as many classical roles as possible,
and by encouraging depictions such as those of Lawrence. That
Kemble wanted to be seen as a true modern proponent of the
ancient world can be proven by his choice of architect for the
rebuilding of Covent Garden in 1808 – of which he was the
manager at the time. Robert Smirke, one of the most rigid of
Greek-revival architects, designed the new building, which was
decorated with sculptures by another classicist, Flaxman. But despite such insistence on the dignity, education and classical knowledge of Kemble, there were others who gave a slightly different
view of his acting and managerial policies. Contemporary comment is especially divergent on the question of Kemble's acting
technique. On his retirement, a critic of the *News* extolled Kemble's
performance of Coriolanus:

It was an epic painting – not of what Rome was . . .; but of the *beau
ideal* of Rome and Coriolanus, which existed in the imagination of

Virgil, of Shakespeare, and of Mr Kemble . . . His manner has often been called classical, probably from his having often acted classical characters, and from loose associations connected with his figure and appearance. But the epithet has a deeper and more appropriate application. His style was *essentially* classical, distinguished by the unity of design, the severe grandeur, and the majestic simplicity which characterized the fine arts of the classic ages.[21]

This critic's view represented one critical opinion of Kemble's style – an opinion echoed by Thomas Lawrence's half-history paintings of the actor. A very different conception appeared in popular prints such as *The Theatrical Ranter* (Plate 7). It shows Kemble in a decidedly unclassical posture and contains the caption 'From – this – day – to – the – end – ing of the world – Ti – Tum – tum – ti – ti – tum – ti', suggesting both awkwardness and monotonous declamation. This negative view of his acting is reinforced by his most vehement critic, Thomas Gilliland, who accused him of 'bleating, grunting, and snuffling through a five act play, like an exhausted post-horse with the hooping cough'.[22]

It is apparent that there was one view of what the stage, and its actors, *should* be and another view of what it actually was. But, so far, this essay has concentrated on writers and artists who were examining the stage critically, and were mining it to defend whatever argument they happened to be presenting. But what about the audience itself, the objects towards which this moralising entertainment was meant to be directed? Certainly the audience responded to the actors and to the plays being presented. The play *Vortigern* (1796) was falsely attributed to Shakespeare, causing a number of different intellectual and critical reactions, including a learned disputation of its authenticity by Edmond Malone. The audience expressed its consideration of the play in a different way, according to Joseph Farington's diary:

> Sturt of Dorsetshire was in a Stage box drunk, & exposed himself indecently to suport the Play, and when one of the stage attendants attempted to take up the green cloth . . . Sturt seized him roughly by the head.[23]

The audience also knew their actors very well and seemed not impervious to the idea that characters could be interpreted in different ways. However, the audience also played favourites, and were not very happy when a new actor took on a role they felt belonged to someone else. The actor Charles Macklin made his fame through a reinterpretation of the character of Shylock, hitherto performed as a low comic character, but elevated by Macklin into a tragic and persecuted figure. However, when Macklin attempted to step out of this role and into the role of Macbeth, he was trespassing on territory that belonged to another actor, 'Gentleman' Smith. Macklin's assumption of the character of Macbeth, and his performance of the role in highland dress, was enough to cause a series of theatrical riots in 1773, leading eventually to his dismissal on 18 November.[24] Macklin felt that a conspiracy had been plotted and that the riots were deliberate. He took certain members of his audience to trial and, two years later, he received his revenge when they were prosecuted. The presiding judge, Lord Mansfield, delivered his verdict with a speech about the reprehensibility of predetermined action in the theatre, suggesting that any audience reaction should be spontaneous.

And usually that was exactly what it was. Audience violence was rarely inspired by a considered critical assessment. More often than not it resulted from an actor's very popularity. For example, in 1794, fifteen people were crushed to death trying to push through the door of the Haymarket, and injury often resulted from too many enthusiastic people wanting to see Garrick at the same time. Sometimes audience disasters had nothing to do with the play at all. At the Haymarket in 1796, according to the *Gentleman's Magazine*, a false fire alarm led to disaster when one gentleman leaped into the orchestra, broke the harpsichord and fractured his skull.[25]

Often such confusion was caused by noblemen to whom the theatre was obviously nothing more than a place one went to if one was a member of Society. Indeed, throughout the century, theatrical hooliganism can often be laid at the door of the class of gentleman to whom humanists were talking when they spoke of moral elevation. For example, on 16 January 1747 the Haymarket was gutted when an advertised performance did not happen. The so-called 'Bottle-Conjuror' was to leap into a wine bottle in front of the amazed eyes of the audience. Although the theatre was full, the Bottle-Conjuror did not appear. The *General Advertiser* quipped 'the only [miracle] he performed was, that he render'd himself invisible . . . to the no small Disappointment of the Gaping

Multitude'.[26] This event inspired a spate of pamphlet literature as well as a satire performed at Bartholomew's Fair the following year called 'Harlequin Jumping Down his Own Throat'. The significant point to make about this event was that the hoax was most likely arranged by the Duke of Montagu and the Duke of Richmond, and the Duke of Cumberland allegedly led the riot.[27]

The play itself, the moral lessons it taught and the useful interpretations of the actors performing in it, were also less important to eighteenth-century theatre audiences than their own self-interest and personal political views. Self-interest was especially apparent when the audience stood to lose something from the theatrical managers. In 1763, for example, a man named Thaddeus Fitzpatrick, described by contemporaries as 'a person of some distinction', led a riot in Covent Garden, creating £2000 worth of damage. He was protesting against a new rule, instituted by the management, that there would be no half-price seats available for those people coming in after the third act. In both 1750 and 1755 riots in the theatre were inspired by troupes of French players, against whom a nationalistic and anti-Jacobite audience objected heartily. The reaction of one member of the audience to the Chinese Festival, performed by French players at Drury Lane in 1755, was polemical and agitational, as an observer reported:

> The leader of the Loyal party advanced to the front of the Gallery and thus bespake the House: 'O Britons! O my countrymen! Ye will certainly not suffer these foreign clogs to amuse us. Our destruction is at hand. These sixty dancers are come over with a design to undermine our constitution. This Navarre is Marshall Lewendahl and the least amongst them is an enseign disguised in order to perpetuate our ruin!'[28]

Politics figured even more strongly towards the end of the century, when the French Revolution fostered divisions in English society as well – divisions which were mirrored in theatrical management at the time. Richard Brinsley Sheridan, the radical MP, was also the manager of Drury Lane Theatre. Kemble was his acting manager from 1788, but there was conflict between the two of them, as Sheridan's political activities were diverting his attention from running the theatre.[29] But it was more than a personality clash; the relationship between Kemble and Sheridan came to be a political one, and came to be seen as such by theatrical audiences.

Kemble's assumption of stately dignity was in part an extension of Burke's ideas about hierarchy and ancient values: one myth perpetuated the idea that Kemble kept a copy of Machiavelli with passages on division and rebellion marked up.

In theatrical terms, the heat of this political clash came to the surface in Sheridan's translation of *Pizarro* (1799), a play by the German dramatist, Kotzebue. Sheridan did little to the play in translation, other than add a few patriotic speeches which were undoubtedly Royalist in their focus. The hero, Rolla, for instance, reminds his troops, 'We serve a monarch whom we love, a God whom we adore,' a sentiment alien to Sheridan's own politics, but destined to bring a lump to the throats of the Drury Lane crowds. Gillray's caricature of Sheridan as Pizarro (Plate 8) spotlights this hypocrisy, just as Dighton's more straightforward print of Kemble as the heroic Rolla (Plate 9), equates that actor with the character who spoke those very sentiments. Kemble's biographer likewise points out the discrepancy:

> There was a political point of no mean importance, obvious in this play; we had Mr Sheridan (formerly furious in the cause of France, invoking destruction upon the heads of the British Cabinet, and coveting for himself the 'blow of vengeance'), now speaking with the heart and voice of his country, his perfect abhorrence of the conduct and the principles of revolution.[30]

The division did not end there. Kemble was also responsible for reviving a long-forgotten play by Havard about Charles I. At the time of the French Revolution the ghost of Charles I came back to haunt the nation, and many compared his fate to that of Louis XVI.[31] Kemble's physical resemblance to the unfortunate King was significantly insisted upon by observers at the time, and his revival of the play was thus particularly timely.

Such parallels may at first seem overly-subtle, but, in the early part of the nineteenth century, the audiences' reactions suggested that these divisions were very real. In 1802 Kemble broke away from Sheridan and took over the management of Covent Garden. Although he lavished funds on transforming Covent Garden into a neoclassical palace in 1808, the interior of the new theatre was more revealing. When the theatre was rebuilt Kemble instituted a number of very unpopular reforms: he increased all the prices, and rented out a third tier of boxes rather than providing a shilling gallery. The less affluent members of the audience were assigned to the pigeon holes (Plate 10), crowded and fetid spaces at the very top of the theatre. These reforms provoked the 'Old Price Riots' (1809), and they were the subject of a number of revealing pamphlets. Several publications condemned Kemble's creation of more boxes as élitist. One tract, entitled *Broad Hints at Retirement*, accused Kemble of trying to combat public dissent by using 'hydrostatic artillery' and warned him:

> Remember, John, whence came thy coffers full,
> But from the pockets of thy friend John Bull.[32]

That Kemble used policing methods to quell the rebellion is obvious from a number of contemporary accounts, including that of the *Examiner*, which reported:

> The Pit has been metamorphosed into a pugilistic arena where all the blackguards of London, the Jew prize-fighters, Bow Street runners, hackney coach helpers and vagabonds returned from transportation have ranged themselves on the side of the managers.[33]

And Kemble's biographer found it requisite, ten years after the event, to defend Kemble's policing methods, using anti-revolutionary sentiments: 'Nothing but the fear of their *lives* will alarm our rabble sufficiently to quiet them'.[34] According to contemporary accounts, this rift resulted in the Whigs supporting Sheridan at Drury Lane and the Tories supporting Kemble at Covent Garden. The moral lessons of the theatre had thus become superseded by the theatre itself: the 'passive' audience found the theatre a medium through which to express its factionalism and political sentiments.

The fact that the theatre had to be justified in the eighteenth and early nineteenth centuries is significant. The increase of wealth and the breakdown of the class system gave many people a greater opportunity for leisure. If time and money were to be spent, it seemed that there were worse ways to spend them than sitting quietly in an audience, accepting the lessons that a piece of theatrical entertainment was teaching you. But the true situation was not so simple. Those foreign visitors who commented on the cruelty and aggression of English leisure activity were not far off the mark. The theatre, too, became a focal point for this aggression and an excuse and justification for the expression of deeper social tensions.

Notes

1. Anonymous, *An Essay on Tragedy, with a Critical Examen of Mahomet and Irene* (London, 1749) p. 2.
2. Jonathan Richardson, *A Discourse on the Dignity, Certainty, Pleasure and Advantage of the Science of a Connoisseur* (London, 1715), pp. 44–5. See also Carol Gibson-Wood, 'Jonathan Richardson and the Rationalisation of Connoisseurship', *Art History*, vol. 7, no. 1 (1984), pp. 38ff.
3. The best general account of 18th-century audiences is Leo Hughes, *The Drama's Patrons: A Study of the 18th-century London Audience* (Austin and London, 1971).
4. Anonymous, *Guide to the Stage* (London, 1750).
5. Anonymous, *The Stage, The Highroad to Hell* (London, 1767), dedication.
6. See Anonymous, *Remarks on the Theatre and on the Late Fire at Richmond in Virginia* (York, 1812); Anonymous, *Christian and Critical Remarks on a Droll or Interlude called the Minor . . . by a Minister of the Church of Christ* (London, 1760); Anonymous, *A Letter to Mr. Foote Occasioned by his Letter to the Rev. Author of the Christian and Critical Remarks* (London, 1760), Anonymous, *The Advantages of Theatrical Entertainment Briefly Considered* (Glasgow, 1772) and Anonymous, *An Address to the Ladies on the Indecency of Appearing at Immodest Plays* (London, 1756) p. 10.
7. See Ronald Paulson, *Hogarth, His Life, Art and Times*, 2 vols (New Haven and London, 1971).
8. *Monthly Mirror* (Feb, 1795).
9. See Shearer West, 'The Theatrical Portrait in 18th-century London', PhD thesis, St Andrews University, 1986; *Royal Opera House Retrospective 1732–1982*, exhibition catalogue (London, 1982); Raymond Mander and Joe Mitchenson, *Guide to the Somerset Maugham Collection of Theatrical Paintings* (London, 1980); *The Georgian Playhouse*, exhibition catalogue (London, Hayward Gallery, 1975).
10. William Cooke, *Elements of Dramatic Criticism* (London, 1775) p. 32.
11. Anonymous, *The Art of Joking; or An Essay on Witticism* (London, 1780) pp. 51–2. See also Oliver Goldsmith, *The Bee* (London, 1759); Abbé Jean Bernard le Blanc, *Lettres d'un François* (Paris, 1745) and René Rapin, *Réflexions sur la poétique d'Aristote* (Paris, 1674).
12. Cooke, *Elements of Dramatic Criticism*, p. 145.
13. William van Lennep (ed.), *The Reminiscences of Sarah Kemble Siddons* (Cambridge, 1942) p. 17. See also William Whitley, *Artists and their Friends in England, 1700–99*, 2 vols (London, 1928) II, pp. 4–6.
14. See Winifred Friedman, *Boydell's Shakespeare Gallery* (New York, 1976).
15. D. E. Williams, *The Life and Correspondence of Sir Thomas Lawrence*, 2 vols (London, 1831), pp. 316–7.

16. James Boaden, *Memoirs of Mrs Siddons*, 2 vols (London, 1827) II, pp. 177–8.
17. See Lance Bertlesen, 'David Garrick and English Painting', *Eighteenth Century Studies*, XI (Spring 1978), pp. 308–24, and Peter Walch, 'David Garrick in Italy', *Eighteenth Century Studies*, III (Summer 1970), pp. 523–31.
18. Anonymous, *An Authentic Narrative of Mr Kemble's Retirement* (London, 1817) p. xxiii.
19. James Boaden, *Memoirs of the Life of John Philip Kemble*, 2 vols (London, 1825) II, p. 432.
20. Boaden, *Kemble*, I, p. 10 and William Cooke, *Memoirs of Samuel Foote*, 3 vols (London, 1805) I, p. 17.
21. *The News* (29 June 1817), quoted in *An Authentic Narrative*, p. 32.
22. Thomas Gilliland, *Elbow Room . . . Containing Remarks on the Shameful Increase of the Private Boxes of Covent Garden* (London, 1804) pp. 11–12.
23. Kenneth Garlick and Angus MacIntyre (eds.), *The Diary of Joseph Farington*, 6 vols (London, 1978) II, p. 518.
24. See Shearer West, 'Zoffany's *Charles Macklin as Shylock* and Lord Mansfield', *Theatre Notebook*, vol. XL, no. 1 (1989), pp. 3–9; James T. Kirkman, *Memoirs of the Life of Charles Macklin*, 2 vols (London, 1799); William Appleton, *Charles Macklin: An Actor's Life* (Cambridge, 1961); *An Apology for the Conduct of Mr Charles Macklin Comedian* (London, 1773).
25. *Gentleman's Magazine* (September 1796).
26. *General Advertiser* (17 January 1747).
27. See George Winchester Stone jnr, *The London Stage, Part 4: 1747–76* (Carbondale, Illinois, 1962) vol. I.
28. Anonymous, *The Dancers Damn'd or the Devil to Pay at the Old House* (London, 1755).
29. Thomas Moore, *Memoirs of the Life of the Right Honourable Richard Brinsley Sheridan* (London, 1825).
30. Boaden, *Kemble*, II, p. 241–2.
31. See, for instance, 'A Comparison Between the Disastrous Reigns of Charles I and Louis XVI', in *A Collection of Miscellaneous Cuttings . . . Relating to the French Revolution* (London, 1791, 1792). See also David Bindman, *The Shadow of the Guillotine: Britain and the French Revolution* (London, 1989).
32. 'A Theatrical Rebel', *Broad Hints at Retirement* (London, 1810) p. 9.
33. *The Examiner* (15 October 1809).
34. Boaden, *Kemble*, II, p. 308–9. For further discussion of these and other issues see Shearer West, *The Image of the Actor: Verbal and Visual Representations in the Age of Garrick and Kemble* (London, 1991) and 'Thomas Lawrence's "Half-History" Portraits and the Politics of Theatre', *Art History*, XIV (June, 1991), pp. 225–49.

7

Harold Abrahams: Athlete, Author and Amateur

John Bromhead

Harold Abrahams was a man of many parts and a man to whom very many people throughout the world have been introduced through the art-form of the film, *Chariots of Fire*[1]. The film is about the 1924 Olympic Games in Paris and about the fortunes of two of Britain's gold medal winners, Eric Liddell (the man who wouldn't run on Sunday) and Harold Abrahams.[2]

First, consider Harold Abrahams, the athlete. The film *Chariots of Fire* is an appropriate starting point. We can, at the same time, consider the effect of the art-form of the film upon the portrayal of a particular leisure activity. One of the best known athletics photographs of all time is of the last strides of the 100 m Final in the Stadium at Colombes in the 1924 Olympic Games. The film-makers have in fact cunningly disguised Bebington Oval, Merseyside, to look as near as possible to the Colombes Stadium of sixty years ago. Moreover, the run round the quadrangle before the clock finished chiming was not done by the real Harold but by Lord Burleigh, and it was a tradition not of Harold's College, Caius, but of Trinity College. In addition it is said, and I underline 'said', that the film-makers were refused the use of Trinity College Great Court, and they therefore filmed the sequence instead at Eton College. For the purpose of further exploring the subject of leisure in the art-form of the film let us consider some of the other distinctly unhistorical sequences in *Chariots of Fire*. Harold did not meet Sybil until later in his life, so probably the main feminine influence in his life in 1924 was his mother. In support of this theory are the fact that Jewish mothers do traditionally have much influence in the family, and a photograph which shows Harold being greeted by his mother (alone) on his return from his triumph in Paris. Harold also records how his mother had to learn of his triumph in Paris in 1924 by listening to the 9.00 p.m. news.

99

Again, it is not a fact that he came home from Paris with a gold medal in his suitcase, as it arrived by post a month later. What is more, the portrayal of the other main character and athlete in the film is also inaccurate. Eric did not just discover that the heats for the 100 m (and incidentally for the 4 x 100 m relay and the 4 x 400 m relay) would be held on a Sunday. Eric had known this months before and plans had all been well laid that he should run the 200 m (in which he came 3rd) and the 400 m which he won with such guts. Here too I should like to mention the influence of Eric's sister, Jenny Somerville, because in real life there was no threat of Eric's athletics taking precedence over his evangelism. The more relevant fact, but a fact that did not suit the film-makers and which has no mileage in any art-form, is that (as she has told me in an interview) the athletics ability of her eldest brother did not interest her at all, and surprisingly she never saw Eric run.

It is interesting to note the success of *Chariots of Fire* – in which Jenny accepted the considerate invitation to play a small acting role. I could list other examples of discrepancies between sports history as seen in *Chariots* and history as it really happened, but I am not the first to point out that these and other fabrications do not matter. The film was in fact extremely well researched and what liberties have been taken are fully justified for dramatic effect – what is known as cinematograph licence. 'It is drama based on fact and faithful to the character, circumstances and driving forces relating to Abrahams and Liddell'.[3] That quotation from a review of the film by Mel Watman fails to point out what a good case there is for saying that there is significant distortion in the character portrayal of Harold Abrahams.

Because these points are central to the theme of leisure in art, and because a probing beneath the surface into some of the complications of an artistic weaving of a tangled web is, I believe, revealing, I shall dwell on this point of character portrayal and possible distortion. It is the off-the-track action contrasting the backgrounds and motivations of Abrahams and Liddell that makes the film interesting, and it was because it was interesting as a work of art rather than as a piece of sports history, however thrilling, that it appealed to such a world-wide audience. I agree with the conclusions that Mel Watman makes to his review, namely that 'Abrahams and Liddell were both, in their differing ways, remarkable men as well as superb athletes and *Chariots of Fire* is a worthy testament to their memory', but his description of Harold as the 'son of a Jewish immigrant from Lithuania . . . spurred on by the genteel anti-semitism he encountered at Cambridge to prove himself a great athlete and be accepted as an Englishman by the Establishment' further entangles some of the distortion woven into the film. The evidence to support this contention comes from two tape recordings made with Harold, one by Rex Alston[4] and one by myself[5] in October 1977, only twelve weeks before Harold died.

Harold was extremely well motivated long before he reached Cambridge. His brother Sydney was a very good 100 m runner and long jumper and he got his Blue at Cambridge. Harold saw Sydney wearing his Blue blazer in 1904 and although Harold was only six years old at the time he knew then that he wanted to get a blazer of his own like the one his brother Sydney had, and to wear it as soon as possible. So firstly, and normally, there was the influence of the parents – and it is well known that the boys' father had made it his ambition that his four sons should go to Cambridge – secondly there was the influence upon Harold of two of his successful elder brothers, Adolphe and Sydney. In later life Adolphe became a successful doctor and Sydney a successful lawyer, and they both received knighthoods. The contention that Harold's motivation was more in response to the examples of his brothers than in reaction to anti-semitism is supported by the known intensity of Harold's desire to be awarded a knighthood like Adolphe and Sydney. However, there is no smoke without fire, and Harold did say to Rex Alston, in the above-mentioned interview, that he did want to prove himself as a man, partly because of the anti-semitism he met at school; but no mention was made of anti-semitism at Cambridge, a significant omission. In a scene near the beginning of the film there is an exchange between Harold and a college porter at Caius College Porters' Lodge in which anti-Jewish innuendoes are in the air. This is probably good film-making and derives its authority from the subtle way it handles nice distinctions in the complicated wickerwork of British social life. However, I do not think it is my love of Cambridge, nor the thirty years that elapsed between Harold's years there and mine, that make me cringe slightly at what I think is a misrepresentation of anti-semitism at Cambridge. By the time English boys reach university some of the power of their nastier attributes has been lost. There is a further point here (which I owe to the late Dr Richard Szreter, my former colleague at Birmingham) which is not irrelevant to a discussion of the niceties, or perhaps they should be called nastinesses, of English society, namely that Harold would have met a lot of so-called 'nobs' at Cambridge and would have had thereby the competitive will to prove himself reinforced.

There is another quotation about Harold's extreme ambition, from an article about David Puttnam, the producer of *Chariots of Fire*, by Tina Brown.[6] The author's comments give further insight into the way in which life – here, specifically, the leisure-life of amateur athletics – changes when it is portrayed in art or, as in this case, in the art-form of the film. When an artist paints a portrait it can usually be said that there is much of the artist in it as well as, hopefully, much of the subject of the portrait. In fact it may be in the mix that a good work of art becomes most interesting. It is usually admitted that in the art-form of photography an exact likeness is being sought, but that in portrait-painting there is usually more interpretation and comment (whether it be flattery, admiration, irritation or some other factor). So too, in her article on David Puttnam, Tina Brown argues that the producer, probably unwittingly, delineated much of his own character in the characters of Abrahams and Liddell as he portrayed them. 'The film Puttnam made, *Chariots of Fire*, was "squeaky-clean".' If you share my liking for the Homeric habit of giving people and things conventional epithets like 'the wine-dark sea' or 'wily Odysseus' or 'the bright-eyed Athene' or 'the white-armed Nausicaa', you may like, in a similar way, to associate the epithet 'squeaky-clean' with *Chariots of Fire*. But that is to speak at a tangent. The film, Tina Brown argues, reconciles two sides of his (Puttnam's) nature:

Abrahams, the Jewish outsider in the Cambridge establishment, competitive, professional, a passionate meritocrat flawed by his fierce desire for glory, is very much a Puttnam figure. Puttnam, half-Jewish and self-made, has always felt intellectually under-estimated. 'I am what I call semi-deprived and Abrahams says, 'They lead me to water, but they won't let me drink.' He is running against anti-semitism and élitism. Liddell, by contrast, is the pure conscience-driven hero who believes his talent is God-given and cannot break his principles to run on the Sabbath. He is running for God. Patsy Puttnam says, ' David is torn between these characters, the man he is versus the man he wants to be.'

A feature of a work of art is that people see different things in it, and, if that is not only a feature but also a criterion of a work of art, then *Chariots* passes the test. The other good thing about this quotation from Tina Brown is that it clarifies for us the characterisation of Harold Abrahams as shown in the film and helps us towards an understanding of Abrahams the athlete.

On the subject of Harold Abrahams as an athlete I have concentrated on the picture of him as depicted in the film *Chariots of Fire*. I have tried to revise that picture where it was historically most misleading – namely in not stressing the intense influence on Harold of his parents and brothers. I have avoided giving a long list of Harold's athletic achievements and have only emphasised the 100 m victory in Paris in 1924, which crowned his efforts. If you listen to the tapes referred to above, you will learn of his first win, on the sands at Hunstanton, for which he won a copy of *Pilgrim's Progress* by John Bunyan, and of his successes at Repton and elsewhere as a junior. In the Oxford versus Cambridge fixture he once won three events in an afternoon, and came down with a total bag of eight gold medals. At Repton he once jumped clean out of the long-jump pit and only failed to beat C. B. Fry's record because the pit had only been cut to twenty feet and as Harold fell back from the edge of the grass his bottom made an imprint on the sand. In C. B. Fry's autobiography it is wrongly stated that Harold broke Fry's twenty-one foot long-jump record.[7] Harold's long-jumping career ended dramatically in 1924 when he broke his leg – an incident which is described in Rex Alston's interview. Rex was present on the occasion and took Harold's place in the sprints, representing Bedfordshire against London Athletic Club at Stamford Bridge. Harold himself says that he was quite relieved at having to retire from athletics under doctor's orders, because he went out at the top and it is hard to improve on an Olympic gold medal in the 100 m. However, before he broke his leg it had been his ambition to be the first Briton to jump twenty-five feet. Before finally leaving the question of athletic ambition and motivation, I should add that in the tape recording given to me Harold commented on the fact that he beat three American sprinters in winning his gold medal; his words, which further modify the relative importance of anti-semitism as a driving force, were; 'I took a great delight in beating Americans, but it was all very childish.' Harold trained three times a week when an undergraduate at Cambridge and employed Sam Mussabini as his coach. For his day, he was a very serious and committed athlete, and if only a guardian angel or goddess had protected him from that fateful injury his list of victories would have been much longer.

A glance at the bibliography of his works[8] only partly shows how active Harold was as an author. For, as well as the published works I have listed, Harold Abrahams did, of course, write many articles for magazines and scripts for broadcasts. For example, in *World Sports* alone in just one (sample) year, 1948, he wrote nineteen articles. The topics he chose to write about were usually themes that keep recurring in athletics, and therefore they are interesting to read although written about forty years ago. Let us look at one of Harold's articles, 'A yardstick for world records' (*World Sports*, 8 March 1948),[9] in which he discussed whether, and in what way, athletics records can be compared. He was interested in the points tables for the decathlon, which covers ten events, for each of which a decathlete is given points which are added up to make a grand total. The question is open for much discussion; for how do you compare statistically a great pole vault with a great shot put or a great mile? Typically Harold milks it, for he is in his element in the world of statistics; he was known as The Father of the National Union of Track Statisticians and was its first President. The international counterpart of the NUTS was founded in a Belgian café by Harold Abrahams (England), Norris McWhirter (Scotland), D. N. Potts (USA) and Roberto Quercetani (Italy). Harold Abrahams was Honorary President (1950). The body was named The Association of Track and Field Statisticians. The article referred to concludes with a discussion of the AAA Standards' Scheme, whereby an award is made to school children who reach a pre-set level of ability at any of the accepted athletics events.

This shows another virtue that Harold had, namely that he was equally at home at all levels of athletics. He liked to point out that he had done every job in athletics – from making the tea to being President. I also got the impression that he did not see the post of President as that of a mere figurehead. Another pet subject about which he wrote with clarity was speed, and the relative speeds of humans, animals and machines. He liked to define human speed as the length of stride times the rapidity of the repetitions. He was an ebullient writer and allowed himself free rein in his chosen fields. In comparing athletics in 1977 with the scene fifty years earlier Harold loved to claim that training was fun in his day. To illustrate this he said that as a student, walking along the pavement, where there was a break in the pavement for a drive entry, he would jump the fifteen-foot gap. This sheer exuberance comes through in his writing. As well as the statistics of the sport,

Harold's interest in photo-finishing and starting often surfaced in his writing. He liked to point out incontrovertible truths, the significance of which might not otherwise have dawned on people. For example, in writing about comparative speeds, and in particular the speed of sound and the speed of radio waves, he said, 'The report from a starter's pistol would be heard by wireless in Australia before it reached a runner standing a few yards away.'[10] It is also typical of Harold and of his output as an author that there was little of importance in athletics that he did not write about somewhere. Long before the names of Abrahams and Liddell were linked in the minds of the public through the film *Chariots*, Harold had already linked them in his role as author. In October 1934 he wrote an article entitled 'Liddell: no Stylist but What a Runner!'.[11] Harold Abrahams was writing for the *Evening Standard* as early as 1920, and he was broadcasting on athletics for the BBC by 1924. It is no over-statement to say that Harold was hated by many members of the National Union of Journalists, because they claimed that, as a freelance writer, he misused his inside knowledge of athlethics gained from the various unpaid posts that he held in the AAA. His answer was that he never betrayed confidences or leaked confidences, and his line was that you should not appoint writers to positions of responsibility in organisations such as the AAA, if you did not expect them to carry on writing. He was a writer before he was an athletics administrator and, though this may partly have been the effect of his life-style, he did not set out to be a breaker of moulds.

Another side to Harold's writing could be labelled his official writing. For example in 1928, as manager of the British team to the Olympic Games in Amsterdam, he wrote the British Olympic Association's official report.[12] In this one suspects that he rather exceeded his brief, with consequences that we shall consider under the heading of Abrahams the Amateur. He was Secretary (the first) of the National Parks' Commission from 1950 to 1963. As part of his official duties in that post he edited a book called *Britain's National Parks*[13] and contributed two of the chapters to that book. For this work as Secretary he was later awarded the C.B.E. How he would have loved to have attracted other honours, particularly from those who are responsible for finalising the lists of those to receive knighthoods. The fact of the matter is that he made too many enemies in the world of athletics in spite of, and even because of, his services to that sport. He was judged, by those who were in a position to know him, to have immeasurably damaged British athletics, mainly because of his opposition to more professional types of national coaching schemes, and through his denial of influence to the national coaches in general and to Geoffrey Dyson in particular. But I should like to end this section on Abrahams as author not on a gloomy note but with a Shakespearian quotation that Harold himself used as a preface to an article of his on speed;[14] it is from *A Midsummer Night's Dream*:

> Oberon: Fetch me this herb, and be thou here again
>   Ere the Leviathan can swim a league.
> Puck: I'll put a girdle round about the earth
>   In forty minutes.

Although Harold was never accepted as a journalist by journalists, he was, as a serious writer on sport, very much accepted by his peers – by, for example, such distinguished writers as Norris McWhirter and Peter Mackintosh. In Harold's copy of Peter Mackintosh's classic book *Sport and Society* there is a hand-written tribute from the author, 'It all stemmed from you really, Harold.'

So finally, we study Harold Abrahams, the amateur. I hope, from what I have said, that you will already have formed some idea of the spirit of the man. It was with this energetic spirit that he tackled the task of writing up the official British Olympic Association report after the 1928 Games. He included in that report a lot about the history of the Olympic Games and a lot about the life of Baron Pierre de Coubertin. I mention this here because this was Harold the amateur historian at work, and he came quite a cropper as the Baron's letter shows.[15] Harold was always fascinated by the subject of amateurism and he would have said 'Amen' to de Coubertin's remarks, in the same letter, that 'there exists no real definition of an Amateur.' In his revising of the IAAF Rule book Harold introduced the word 'subvention', as a term for what an amateur athlete is allowed to accept. Harold said, jovially, that it was a good word because no one knew what it meant. I do not think that one should read too much into that and argue that he was obscurantist, but I see it as a sign of how much he loved amateurism and how reluctant he was to concede defeat and bow to the inevitable. This is not the place to attempt an authoritative verdict on whether Harold betrayed his own amateur ideals by cashing in on his success as a sprinter, but I would contend that, by his hatred of the idea that the main or only motivation to excel in athletics should be financial gain, he has been the mouthpiece for a very lively and fun-loving streak in the British character. This gentlemanly approach is highlighted when it is in stark contrast to the typically American predilection for a winner. There are at least three ironies in this saga. First, Harold, who championed the amateur cause, employed Sam Mussabini as his professional coach before the days when this was the general practice. The second irony is that he beat three Americans in the Final of the 1924 Olympic Games 100 m with a determination to win that is more often associated with the Americans than with the British. The third irony underlines how misleading this division between amateur and professional can be. I refer to the fact that Harold Abrahams, the so-called champion of amateurism, was himself the upholder of the highest professional standards (in the best sense of that phrase).

We have considered three aspects of the personality of Harold Abrahams and in the reading have discovered a little about leisure in art and literature. I would like to end by referring again to the film *Chariots of Fire*, because it is the impact of this very professional film which has kept the name of Harold Abrahams before the public. It can hardly be said too often that from motives of personal gain or national power, political or commercial, film, video or media barons will want to tamper with and distort history. There are times to call a halt to such proclivities, but I submit that although the film *Chariots of Fire* is not historically accurate it explicitly does not set out to be such, and I have not met anyone who felt that the inaccuracies of the film in any way detracted from its appeal as a work of art.

Notes

1. The film *Chariots of Fire*, (1981) broke all Box-Office records for a foreign film shown in the USA and won an Oscar in 1981 for 'The best film'.
2. D. P. Thomson, *Eric H. Liddell, Athlete and Missionary* (The Research Unit, Crieff, 1971). S. Magnusson, *The Flying Scotsman* (London, 1981).
3. M. Watman, 'Chariots of Fire: a Thrilling and Moving Film', *Athletics Weekly*, (25 April 1981) pp. 21–22.
4. R. Alston, 'People To-day' (London, 1963).
5. H. M. Abrahams, 'NCAL Tapes 24 & 25' (Birmingham, NCAL, 1977).

6. T. Brown. 'The End of the Affair', *Sunday Times Magazine* (24 April 1988), pp. 24–38.
7. C. B. Fry, *Life Worth Living* (London, 1934).
8. J. N. Bromhead *A Bibliography of Works by Harold Abrahams* (NCAL XXV.H27), (unpublished).
9. H. M. Abrahams, 'A Yardstick for World Records' *World Sports*, XIV, no. 3 (London, 1948) pp. 8–9.
10. H. M. Abrahams, 'Speed', *World Sports XV*, no. 1 (London, 1949) pp. 12–13.
11. H. M. Abrahams, 'Liddell no Stylist, but What a Runner!' *Athletics Weekly* (17 April 1982) pp. 25–26.
12. British Olympic Association, *Official Report of the IXth Olympiad, Amsterdam 1928* (London, 1928).
13. H. M. Abrahams (ed.), *Britain's National Parks* (London, 1959).
14. W. Shakespeare, *A Midsummer Night's Dream*, II. i. 172–5.
15. P. de Coubertin (Baron), 'Observations on 1928 BOA Official report, 1930', (NCAL VII, 1928) (The Library of the University of Birmingham).

8

'To the Glory that was Greece': Classical Images in Public School Athleticism

Malcolm Tozer

It was John Stuart Mill who once remarked that the Greeks were the initiators of nearly everything, Christianity excepted, of importance in the western world, and no study of nineteenth-century English education can ignore them. Throughout the Victorian and Edwardian éras the two classical languages, Latin and Greek, dominated the curriculum of the public schools – generally taking more than half of the available classroom time. Most schoolmasters had read classics at the ancient universities, and as late as 1914, 92 of the 114 public school headmasters were classicists.[1] Much earlier, Thomas Arnold, the headmaster of Rugby from 1828 to 1842, had brought in two important innovations to the teaching of classics, which had increased their popularity: first, he shifted the balance away from Latin and towards Greek; and secondly, he used a mix of classics and history and applied it to explain contemporary social and political problems.[2] Arnold's reforms were soon to extend to most public schools, and after 1840 the classical pendulum stayed firmly in the Greek sector. Thus the ideas of the ancient Greeks, suitably filtered at school for adolescent consumption, gradually came to provide the philosophical grounding and the mystical support for all shades of Victorian opinion; and though only a tiny minority of the nation might learn Greek – and only a small minority of them took their studies seriously – the influence of the reading men was soon to be most persuasive.

The Greeks did not have just one school of thought on educational matters; in Athens and Sparta, for example, we have two highly contrasting ideals, though both drew support from the same epics of Homeric times. The beauty of Greece is that each subsequent philosophy can find at least one Greek model to serve as a platform on which its own developments can be built, and in this manner Athens, Sparta and Homeric Greece can each be shown to have its own golden age in the years between 1840 and 1918. The public schools at the beginning of this period owe much to Platonic Athens; the emergence of athleticism would seem to belong more to Sparta; whilst the age of imperialism at the end of our period has a decidedly Homeric flavour. It is a curiosity that, as nineteenth-century public school educational practice evolved, so it sought support from earlier and more primitive Greek models.

Platonic influence on all our thinking about the practical conduct of life has been, and still is, incalculable: if we sometimes underestimate our debt to Plato in these matters it is only because his ideas have become so completely part and parcel of our best traditions. Much of this stems from the early Victorians, who felt a special kinship with the Athens of the last years of the fifth century BC, and they repeatedly looked to this past for the keys to their own problems. There are many similarities between the Athenian democracy and early Victorian England: both were maritime nations, and both had gained security after triumph in war – Trafalgar and Waterloo matching Salamis and Marathon; and both had growing empires on which undoubted commercial success was built. In name both societies were democracies, though in each case the democratic rights were shared by only a few; in both, the social imbalance was partly redressed by genuine service given to the state by the ruling aristocratic families; and both ruling classes were civilised and cultured, with each giving considerable attention to the arts. In Victorian England Plato was, remarkably, the gospel for Utilitarians and Radicals, and for Tractarians and Evangelicals: all drew on his educational thought as expounded in the *Republic*.

The Platonic ideal of the beautiful and the good, though it was realised for less than 80 years, left behind it an imperishable memory. The exemplar possessed all the desirable physical, intellectual, aesthetic and moral capacities and gifts, and they were tuned in perfect harmony: he was the whole man.[3] The revival of this philosophy as the basis of Hellenism occurred in Rome in Christian times, and then passed into the Western Church. In England Plato became the intellectual source for all Anglican theology from Hooker onwards – bar a short eclipse under the Puritans – and by the beginning of the nineteenth century it had become the life-blood of romanticism.[4] Ogilvie has noted the re-orientation of classics from Latin to Greek in this period, and especially to the philosopher Plato and the historian Thucydides. At the universities the changeover came in the 1830s, when Sewell began to lecture in Cambridge on the *Republic*; Oxford followed suit in 1847 when Jowett lectured on Plato. We have seen Arnold's influence at Rugby, and the same picture emerges from the Shrewsbury of Butler and Kennedy, from Prince Lee's King Edward's, Birmingham, and from Thring's Uppingham. Greek became the staple diet in early Victorian public schools.[5] As the century progressed, so the Platonists came to the fore. The poets Wordsworth and Browning exude his message, and Carlyle admired the ideal of service; Coleridge was probably the greatest of the Platonic philosophers, he in turn inspired Maurice, Tennyson and Hare; Kingsley thought Plato the king of the philosophers, and Ruskin would read from his works every day; and, of the later poets, Cory and Matthew Arnold are but two who glorified Platonism in their writings.[6]

Virtually all idealistic theories of education can be traced back to Plato's *Republic*, where the aim is to produce ideal citizens to play their part in the ideal community. Service was the corner-stone of this community, for within an ordered society each citizen would disinterestedly concede his own preferment and would loyally serve others. Plato was convinced that happiness was the reward of virtue, and that the virtuous life was the only pleasant one. It was not the having of strength, long life, health or wealth, but the right use of them that made men happy. Here education had its role, and the method was to surround the child with objects and examples worthy of imitation.[7] The concept of the whole man was based on a balance of the appetitive, spirited and philosophic elements of a man's soul. The appetitive element was concerned with the pursuit of bodily desires, and was an animal rather than a human quality. The spirited element was the source of courage and self-confidence, whilst the philosophic involved intellect and all learning: an education in 'gymnastic' and 'music' would develop them. The balance of the three elements was essential in the whole man, and this harmony Plato termed *arete* – interpreted by Nicolson as 'balanced achievement'.[8] The soul was to aspire to three virtues – truth, courage and self-control – and as these were to become the three ingredients of the mid-Victorian ideal of manliness let us use contemporary sources to find their meaning. Truth implied all honest action, truth to oneself and truth to one's loyalties; courage had animal bravery as its base but rose to fortitude under affliction and in adversity – it was also the courage of men loyal to their principles; self-control was obedience to authority, whether the authority of a ruler or of one's higher inner self.[9] Platonic education came through 'music' and 'gymnastic'. 'Music' included literature, music and the visual arts, and it was central to Plato's philosophy that beauty in nature and art was but an outward sign of goodness. 'Gymnastic' aimed at simplicity of life and diet, and the maintenance of good health. 'Music' and 'gymnastic' did not separately educate the philosophic and spirited elements of the soul, but were finely tuned to produce the perfect harmony of the whole man.

Arnold was the first public school headmaster who tried to put Platonic theory into practice, and at Rugby in the 1830s education became the cure of souls. Now Platonic philosophy, Christianity and educational practice became inseparable: education was merely that aspect of moral training concerned with childhood, whereas religion was the application of this way of life to all ages.[10] Arnold's synthesis of all social and religious problems helped to root the Church firmly on earth and to direct its attention to earthly reality. Arnold's success was sure: classics in the classroom became more relevant and palatable, service to others was instilled through the prefectorial system, and the chapel sermon provided the medium for the message. Here is the first school as a microcosm of Plato's Republic. Now Arnold's methods spread – first through the actions of Rugby schoolmasters or of Arnold's pupils who became headmasters of other schools, and secondly through the broadening of the message by the Christian Socialists.

The ideal society that Arnold strove towards at Rugby gained wider meaning through the efforts of the Christian Socialists in the years between 1848 and 1852. Under the leadership of Maurice, Kingsley and Hughes many young men at the universities were drawn to a movement that sought to improve the living and working conditions of the nation's poor: now Platonic service was extended beyond the boundary of the school. Evening schools, mechanics institutes, Bible classes, country outings, boxing and football became commonplace, and many of the men who ran these activities became the schoolmasters for the next generation.[11] Kingsley and Ruskin did not enter the classroom, but by their efforts at Eversley and Hinksey and through their popular writings they spread the Platonic message far and wide.[12]

It was now a buoyant time for the public schools: old foundations were transformed in the Arnoldian image, ancient grammar schools were revitalised by enterprising headmasters, and new schools were created for the expanding middle classes. And no period was more blessed with headmasters: able men, nursed in the Romantic tradition, brought intellectual drive, moral certainty and spiritual conviction to their schools. Great headmasters went on to become great men, with two, Benson of Wellington and Temple of Rugby, following in succession as Archbishops of Canterbury. Individually and severally these men brought to fruition the mid-Victorian ideal of manliness: the efforts of Benson and Temple are well recorded, Harper of Sherborne or Ridding of Winchester could serve as our guides, but for convenience let Thring be our idealist in practice.[13]

Thring came to the small country grammar school at Uppingham in 1853, and he quickly transformed it into a well-known boarding school of some 300 boys. In the manner of his contemporary headmasters, but with greater zeal than most, he applied the Platonic tradition that he had absorbed at Cambridge to the practical running of his school. Lessons in classics were rooted in Greek literature and the history of Thucydides, and were applied to more modern problems; the beauty of art was brought into the classrooms, and the beauty of nature was studied in the countryside; Christian guidance and hope were offered from the pulpit; gardening, an aviary, workshops and music made an environment worthy of emulation; and life in the homely boarding houses instilled a sense of communal responsibility and a spirit of individual freedom.[14]

True to the Platonic tradition Thring was sure that physical prowess rightly used was a powerful weapon for good, and he sought to devise a system to inculcate such qualities and habits in his pupils. Thring, a true country parson's son, enjoyed robust living, and generations of Uppinghamians became used to a life of simple fare and few comforts, steeplechase runs and dips in the rivers, and early morning school. Timetabled gymnastics classes were instituted to improve strength and agility and to foster a broad repertoire of physical skills; swimming was taught, and boys were encouraged to take the tests in life-saving for the Royal Humane Society's medal; and the many events and the several weeks of the athletics sports were devised to push each boy to the limits of speed, strength and endurance. Games had long been played at Uppingham, as elsewhere, but now they too were harnessed for their educational worth. The informal play of the past was now codified, so that regular matches could be played, and funds were made available for the provision of pitches and courts, clothing and equipment, trophies and travel. Coaching was minimal, for the benefits to physical development, social training and moral guidance would come with the bumped balls and dropped catches, the bruising tackles and the missed goals, no matter how well or how badly the games were played. The whole physical education process – and it deserves such a label since it was there by design and it was directed at all pupils – was an integral part of the overall educational plan.[15] At the basic level there was a need for a sound physique and a range of physical skills; above that came a training in truth, courage and self-control; and finally came a recognition of the needs of others and of service to the community. Such a physical education could thus contribute its part – along with, for example, the chapel, classics, the boarding house and the arts – to the overall moral training. On leaving school a boy would thus be ready to serve his fellow men in city slums, industrial mills or country parishes. This message Thring would readily and regularly ply from the pulpit as he pointed out to his charges how life at Uppingham was, in every respect, geared to prepare them for earthly service to Christ.[16]

All this came to be called muscular Christianity, and its heyday was the period from 1850 to 1870. These were the years of Platonic Athens when reforming cleric-headmasters built a nation of Republics on Christian foundations. The ancient ideal of the whole man had become the ideal of manliness, and through a hardy but homely dose of Thucydides and gymnastics, divinity and country rambles, chapel sermons and football matches, several generations of public schoolboys were inspired to go out into the world and serve their fellow men.[17]

But the athletic means to a moral end was now to become an end in itself. This change began in all innocence with the understandable enjoyment of this novel aspect of school life instilling over-enthusiasm amongst its supporters; but soon the new athletic lobby began to pull on the ideal of manliness and eventually separated it from its Platonic roots. The Clarendon Report and *Tom Brown's Schooldays* were at the beginning of the process. In 1860

'Paterfamilias' in a letter to the *Cornhill Magazine* opened a controversy on the quality of education at the public schools that was to lead to the creation of the Public Schools Commission under Lord Clarendon. He complained that though the schools, and Eton in particular, were sound academically they provided no moral training: by the time of the publication of the report in 1864 a remedy had been found – games were to provide the moral training, and the commissioners advocated that much time should be devoted to these activities. Thus games swept ahead of the other moral trainers in the curriculum and the moral virtues to be gained from athletic exercise were loudly proclaimed.[18] In *Tom Brown's Schooldays* Hughes hoped to portray Rugby in Arnold's time, but instead his readers enjoyed a boyish romp that glorified everything athletic in school life from fisticuffs to football. The hero became a good Christian largely by physical means; and in Tom the three Platonic virtues were no longer equally balanced, for a self-reliant, high-spirited courage now came to the fore.[19] To keen games players the competition inherent in all sport seemed to gain respectability from Darwin's newly published evolutionary theories and from Spencer's twist of social evolution; whilst Spencer's warning of the survival of the fittest matched the sense of progress of the era and helped bring about the athletic tilt of the mid-Victorian ideal of manliness.[20] Cotton at Marlborough and Vaughan at Harrow had successfully used organised games and young, athletic masters to bring discipline to unruly schools, and there was no doubt that sporting glory was a more powerful advertisement than the published headmasterly sermons of the previous decades.[21]

The floodgates opened – all schools would play games. In this era of the most rapid expansion of the public school system the basic formula for a successful school was derived. It should be a self-contained society, partly self-governing and partly ruled by an autocratic headmaster. The aim of its education was less in intellectual qualities and more in terms of leadership and the arts of social ascendancy: it was in this latter aspect that games were to play their part. The end product was the Christian gentleman personified by Tom Brown. As each new school came about, so the games ethos was more readily accepted and soon the older foundations followed suit – usually reacting to the pressure of senior boys at the school and young old boys at the universities.[22] Private school games were summarily abolished, sometimes by the boys, sometimes by the headmaster: marbles, peg-top, skipping, hop-scotch and the like were quickly replaced by football – usually the Rugby variety – cricket and rowing. Soon the tail was wagging the dog as boys at most schools clamoured for cups and colours, house competitions and school matches, resident professionals and better facilities; within a few years games alone determined the status of a boy, and the position of his school in the national rank-order.[23]

Almond's Loretto proudly exhibited its athletic prowess. Between 1867 and 1878 Almond built an Anglicised public school in Scotland on the foundation that to keep the body in the best possible condition was a point of conscience and a matter of religion. Discipline was strict; loafers were not tolerated; caning for minor offences was exercised by prefects, and switching with the birch for serious ones by Almond. Matters physical dominated school life, scholarship was definitely secondary, and the arts hardly existed. The equation of life was simple: fresh air, personal cleanliness, careful diet, regular hours, sensible dress and physical exercise would combine to produce manliness. Dormitory windows were thrown open at night, cold baths were taken in the morning, and a hardy uniform of tweed trousers and woolen jumpers clothed the boys during the day. The importance of games as moral agents was so vital that Almond invented Loretto time, fifteen minutes ahead of Greenwich, to give more time for their play; and if it was too wet for games then long and arduous cross-country grinds, conducted on a basis of personal trust, took their place. The school's athletic renown was soon formidable, and for the rest of the century old boys gained far more than their share of places in Oxbridge and international teams at Rugby football. Almond's ideal of manliness blended the physical qualities of muscular Christianity with the scientific rationalism of Spencer, and at no time was there a Romantic or Platonic influence. In his sermons Almond preached that to be manly was to be physically able, and that through physical activity the virtues of courage, temperance and team spirit could be felt: this is a Sparto-Christian ideal.[24]

Heartiness was also in vogue south of the border, where men like Stephen and Cory, who had enjoyed the sporting side of the Christian Socialist activities, now sought to promote games for the middle classes. In the early 1860s Stephen did much for athletics at both Oxford and Cambridge, whilst at Eton the boost in games-playing owed much to Cory's influence.[25] Cricket at Eton came to prominence under Mitchell's tutelage from 1865 and, under his watchful eye, it kept its favoured position right to the end of the century. Mitchell was perhaps the first ever games master, being appointed to the staff primarily because of his athletic prowess: he was not the last.[26] The classicist, Warre, had charge of rowing from 1860 until he succeeded to the position of headmaster in 1884, and his contemporaries were sure that his coaching success had positively helped his advancement.[27] Harrow was not to be outdone, and from 1860 until 1901 Bowen guided the school's course in athleticism, vigorously encouraging plain living and simple fare, cold baths and morning swims, team games and racquet sports.[28] Bowen and Cory, like Thring before them, brought poetry and song on the side of the new manliness: Cory's 'Eton Boating Song' and Bowen's 'Forty Years On' being still sung to this day. And each, like Stephen, gradually lost his Christian faith, giving substance to the belief that games were the new religion.[29] Almond's Sparto-Christianity had now become pure Spartanism.

This was the pattern of the times. The erosion of belief had begun under the influence of the Utilitarians, but it was in the wake of Darwin that it accelerated. In the battle of biblical truth against scientific evidence distinguished churchmen found themselves on opposing sides: much of the poetry of Tennyson and Matthew Arnold epitomises the mingled doubt and hope, the dejection and determination of contemporary society. Science brought a chill to the very belief in orthodox religion, especially between 1862 and 1877, when the conflict was at its most bitter. As we move towards the end of the century so headmasters found it progressively more difficult to appoint professedly Christian masters, and soon, too, came the lay headmaster.[30]

The passion for games, checked in the 1860s, now became widespread. Inter-school rivalry increased, and school magazines logged the records of their rivals as well as their own; London matches drew great crowds and could affect the duration of the social season; compulsion operated in the schools, and it was an unusual boy who was not swept along by the athletic craze. What did the headmasters hope to achieve from this headlong dash? Some, in the manner of Cotton and Vaughan, needed to impose discipline on reluctant schools; most saw games as the one area of school life where boys and masters could congenially mix; health was found to improve, and the discomforts and hard knocks that are always part of games had important moral worth. Games were sure to instil glowing spirits, quick obedience, good temper, fair play, self-reliance, endurance, confidence in comrades, ambition, quick judgement, unselfishness, courage and self-control; and the combination of games, the hardy life and a cold bath was the certain antidote to homo-erotic vice.[31] These were the qualities that were to serve the public school old boys well as they went off to the remotest corners of the British Empire – as missionaries, administrators, merchants or soldiers; these were the qualities the recruiting agencies sought.

But service to the Empire needed more than this: a training in team spirit, or *esprit de corps*, would bind the far-flung and isolated subalterns and sahibs to the common cause. Life in the boarding house at school provided the framework, and team games gave the means. The school day became more regimented as free time dwindled; restriction to bounds tightened and freedom to roam the countryside was curtailed; fagging schooled youngsters in obedience, prefecthood their seniors in command. Hughes had earlier suggested the alliance of team games and *esprit de corps* in *Tom Brown's Schooldays*, but it was in the 1870s that it first received general acclaim.[32] If games were to inculcate *esprit de corps*, then they had to be selected carefully and adapted accordingly: individual games such as tennis, gymnastics and golf would have no part, and these activities were generally suppressed in the interests of cricket or football. Hockey, in these early days of play on football pitches, was hard to make a truly team game, so it was regarded as effeminate, fit only for malingerers, or perhaps valuable as a change in hot weather.[33] Cricket can hardly be described as a true team game in the *esprit de corps* sense, but its tradition was long-standing and beyond reproach. It was thus left to football and rowing to produce the ideal. Rowing, with success dependent on the individual acting in concert with his fellows, was the perfect sport, though only a few schools had the good fortune to stand on suitable rivers. Football had no such problem, and its adoption was almost universal. In the earlier period many schools played their own blend of football, but during the 1860s and 1870s most opted for one of the two nationally accepted codes, Association or Rugby, and this led to a marked increase in inter-school matches. Most of the newer or raised schools opted for the Rugby version, and as professional soccer began to taint the gentlemanly image so some of the older foundations followed suit. At most schools, then, the mantle of *esprit de corps* fell on Rugby football. Up until the 1860s the aim of each player in a match had been to take the ball as far upfield as possible by his own play: only when he was tackled or brought to a halt did he pass the ball to a team-mate, and then he too would plough forward. When Almond suggested to the boys at Loretto that they should pass the ball before the tackle was made, his horrified pupils immediately complained that such action was unmanly. Now all this was to change. In the early 1880s Oxford teams developed 'the passing game', as it was christened, and with it, for a number of years, successfully defeated Cambridge, still doggedly ploughing forward. This passing game was soon in use at Cheltenham and Loretto, and within a few years it had spread to other schools.[34] As a true team game, in which success could depend on the weakest player and where much of the best work was done out of sight, and thus unsung, in the scrum, Rugby football was universally extolled as the team game *par excellence*.

A cursory examination of old team photographs from 1850 to 1890 illustrates the change. At the beginning of the period the random grouping of the players and the variety of hairstyle, dress and sporting equipment suggest a carefree atmosphere in the schools; whereas in the later years the sitters are precisely and symmetrically placed in stereotyped poses, and the dress and even the expressions look identical. Here is a visual record of *esprit de corps*; a willingness to belong to a group, the concealment of all personal emotion, and the cultivation of the stiff upper lip – and it was proclaimed as the new manliness. In as much as it made the least member of the school share identity with the cleverest scholars and the athletic heroes, it had its good points; but in the sublimation of the individual to the group norm, the disdain for everything aesthetic, the fear of bad form, and the moulding of personality to the dominant hearty type, the effect was stultifying. To cultivate the individual became to encourage the crank, and this was disloyalty to the tribe.

What had been Platonic Athens was now Sparta. The Spartans of ancient times were the first Hellenic people to emerge from the mists of the Homeric era, and by 600 BC, when Athens was a mere village, Sparta ruled supreme.[35] In Spartan society the individual was submerged in the system, and the state possessed the person – body and soul. Obedience to authority was absolute, with flogging the unwavering response for the slightest offence or the smallest failing. Sparta had come to prominence through war, and it maintained its advantage by devoting all its energies to self-preservation. Here was a city of soldiers – conservative in outlook, suspicious of outsiders and foreigners, and dismissive of all arts and philosophy. Personal comfort and all softness were held in contempt, and a virtue was made of the adoption of all enforced necessities.[36] A hardy martial education was devised, with wrestling and athletics in the curriculum, and throughout this era Spartan athletes dominated the competitions at the Olympic games.[37] For Spartans courage was the sole virtue, and obedience an unswerving habit: Simonides' words on the memorial at Thermopylae to the soldiers who died there in battle serve as the epitaph for a people: 'Stranger, tell the Spartans how we die: obedient to their laws, here we lie.[38] In essence it could also serve for the Eton and Harrow cricketers of the late 1880s, who played in front of 15,000 partisan supporters at Lord's in an atmosphere more akin to a feud or a vendetta than to a sporting contest. An Etonian present later recalled that even in the refreshment intervals the two sets of boys had to be accommodated in separate rooms.[39] Spartan ideals prevailed – two schools, Loretto and Sedbergh, took for their mottoes: 'You have won Sparta, adorn her.'

Esprit de corps may have had some success in bringing the weakling and the dullard to play a fuller part in the life of the school community, but it was much more difficult to contain the athletic hero. The exemplar of the earlier Platonic ideal of manliness was just as likely to be a modest poet as a member of the cricket eleven – and he might be both – but the exemplars of Spartanism had to be the sportsmen. Almond forbade cheering for the individual at matches, instead boys were encouraged to shout for the school; all forms of individual statistics, whether averages in cricket or winners in athletics, were discouraged: by these means, and in a small school, where the headmaster's personal influence was immense, he had some success in curtailing the hero-worship of the star performers.[40] The approach at Clifton was to encourage spectators at matches to applaud the efforts of their opponents as much as they cheered their own side; but most schools either gave up the struggle or tried to legitimise the deification of the athlete.[41] The years from 1890 were the golden age for the hero as a gladiator. A boy's chief ambition on entering a school was likely to be to distinguish himself at games; the swiftest way to eminence in the house or school community was through prowess on the playing fields; and the leading boys, including most of the prefects, were chosen from the prominent performers. Boys, old boys, parents and staff agreed that games were the vital central feature of school life. Thus began in earnest the rule of the 'blood' and the 'hearty' as the talented athletes assumed, with or without the consent of their masters, responsibility for the running of the school; and even when the effects of the reign were seen in the undermining of discipline and the lowering of morality – the earlier reasons for encouraging athleticism – the ideal of *esprit de corps* remained intact and so maintained the status quo. Such was its all-enveloping ethos.[42]

The product of the system was clearly doing well, whether as a soldier on the northwest frontier of India, a district officer in the Straits Settlements of Malaya, or a missionary and teacher in Uganda; and the cry came for more of the same. In the years before 1880 a quiet imperial idealism had been based on a federation of the English-speaking white races, and on service to the backward peoples of Asia and Africa – it was an imperial extension of the brotherhood of the Christian Socialists.[43] Now came a noisier strain. As a consequence of the new power of the united Germany and the industrial might of the emerging United States, Britain in the late 1880s was seen to lose some of its lead over other world powers. This, together with episodes like Gordon's martyrdom in Khartoum and the subsequent denting of British pride, led directly to an era of aggressive acquisition of territory in the scramble for colonies. Africa became the main attraction and, under a cover of doctrines on national destiny and civilising mission, crudely married to policies on materialistic need, the continent was carved up by the world powers. Soon the Far East and the Pacific brought new acquisitions to the British Empire, and by 1899 the total global area under the British flag was equivalent to four Europes, had a population of some 400,000,000, and provided half the world's seaborne trade. Back at home the empire was the paychest for many, and a colonial caste of former planters, merchants, adventurers and soldiers became a powerful influence. Many of these returning expatriates developed strong links with public schools: some retired to the spa towns where many schools were sited; others helped in the foundation of new imperially-minded institutions; and many, as parents, selected for their sons schools that flew imperial colours.

At Victoria's accession to the throne in 1837 hardly a thought was given to the empire; at the Golden Jubilee the emphasis was on civilising mission and duty; the Diamond Jubilee of 1897 became an orgy of self-congratulation and national assertion. Crude, rumbustious, imperial fever intoxicated the nation in the last years of the century, and this sentiment carried all shades of political and religious opinion in its wake. Whether trumpeted by the newly founded *Daily Mail*, imbibed in the verses of Newbolt and Kipling, or sung in such patriotic songs as 'Another Little Patch of Red' or 'Soldiers of the Queen', the hysteria of imperialism swept the country. An expanding empire needed not only administrators and merchants to tap its wealth, but also an army and navy to keep what was held and to conquer what could be gained: as the century closed so more than a million men were in the armed services.[44]

The officers came largely from the public schools, and the regiment or the ship was seen as the natural extension of the boarding house or the cricket eleven: the services could be portrayed as the ultimate in *esprit de corps*.[45] With 30,000 boys in the public schools of 1900, there were more boys than ever; and there were more schools to accommodate them. Much of the increased custom came from the *nouveaux riches* whose wealth derived from the empire; still more profit came from a genre of literature spawned from *Tom Brown's Schooldays* but now set in the fictional world of Monkshall or St Mark's. Countless tales mixed schoolboy adventures with athletic glories, and led to daring deeds in the empire: each helped to keep alive the sporting ethos, to prepare the next generation of aspiring public schoolboys, and to spread the ideal to the thousands of boys who would never go near such a school, but who would feel its influence secondhand through the scouting movement or one of the other youth groups. The poets played their part too: Henley's stirring collection of Union Jack verse, aptly titled *Lyra Heroica*, was distributed at countless prize-givings, and Newbolt's 'Vitaï Lampada', with its linking of cricket on 'a bumping pitch and a blinding light' to battle in a distant land where 'the Gatling's jammed and the Colonel's dead', helped to cement the relationship between sport at school and military service in the empire – evocatively reinforced with the call to '"Play up! Play up! and play the game!"'.[46]

The Boer War, at the turn of the century, brought the first real test for the athletic-military product – and it was found wanting. Grand-scale warfare against a civilised and vigorous opponent proved more difficult than local military successes against hill-tribesmen in India or Zulu warriors in Africa had suggested it might be, and it took an embarrassed Britain much effort to gain the eventual victory. Kipling's biting criticism of the unprepared and naïve army officers as 'flannelled fools' and 'muddied oafs' stung, but his suggestion that the nation's youth should undergo military training was eagerly adopted.[47] Cadet corps had been founded at some public schools in the 1860s but many, including Uppingham and Loretto, had resisted their introduction. The innovation did not carry much weight, for all corps were voluntary, and their standing figured well below that of team games: cranks might take it seriously, but the real hearties played Rugby football. The change was sudden. Warre, corps commander turned headmaster at Eton, persuaded his fellow headmasters to take immediate action, and in quick succession 83 of the 102 schools contacted either revived and enlarged old corps, or specifically created new ones.[48] Boer War heroes toured the schools to support the initiative; field days, reviews and war games proliferated; attendance at the weekly parades was virtually compulsory; and all the moral virtues formerly attached to games were suddenly transferred to the corps. This was the twentieth-century training in *esprit de corps*. Selwyn was Thring's successor at Uppingham, and his answer to Warre's cry was prompt and whole-hearted. At the start of the first term of the new century he announced that all boys, whether in the corps or not, were required to pass a shooting test, and that no one would be allowed to take part in an athletic contest, nor could he gain a school prize, until that qualification had been acquired.[49] A month later Jones, the commanding officer of the corps, left for active service in South Africa, and his exploits were reported in the school magazine in gory detail.[50] Thring's Platonic ideals had now become 'to fear God, to speak the truth, and to shoot straight'.[51]

It was an heroic age: brave deeds were being performed in South Africa; the writings of Henty, Vachell, Newbolt, Kipling, Buchan and the like all resound to the adventures of men ready to risk all, death included: it became natural to venerate the hero at school. Now the bloods were in the XV *and* in the corps; their rule was absolute.[52] School life was thoroughly regimented; sacerdotalism and ceremony abounded; headmasters – laymen increasingly – were regarded as awesome and unapproachable; religious worship was no more than hearty hymn-singing; and an atmosphere akin to militarism was abroad.[53] These years saw the destruction of the individual boy and his absorption into the group type. Behaviour was governed by 'good form', producing a healthy, good-mannered type, but philistine in taste and without moral fervour: religion was less important than the code of the gentleman or the materialism and snobbery of the *nouveaux riches*.

The emphasis on the classics was as strong as ever, but Plato was almost unread as Homer became the fashionable author. The swift turn-around occurred in the 1890s, and by 1900 all schools read Homer, whilst men as diverse as Warre, Lawrence and Buchan were all enthusiasts.[54] The eighth-century BC poems of Homer record the legends and myths of the Greek heroic age, one that lasted for about four generations and ended in the battle of Troy.[55] The *Odyssey* and the *Iliad* are almost exclusively concerned with the deeds of aristocrats, for the main function of the ordinary man was to be killed by his superiors. The Homeric hero fought for his own glory, and only in later Spartan times did the worthy cause displace personal honour as the prime-mover. Homeric *arete* was equivalent to honour, but such honour bore little resemblance to its Christian and chivalric successors. Honour came with the evidence of the hero's worth, which in turn stemmed from how much glory he had won, and was reflected in his demeanour, his manners, and his dress. The Greek for hero originally meant a warrior, and the hero's status depended on the quality of his opponent, his manner of fighting, and the result of the contest. The heroic qualities thus included high courage, modesty and courtesy; prizes gained were lasting evidence of glory, and were to be displayed on all appropriate occasions; and grand ceremonies would proclaim the hero's virtues.[56] The Edwardians found many parallels between the heyday of the British Empire and the Homeric legends of the past, and saw their own society as the new heroic age.

Heroes are trained for war, and here too the classics brought support – acting like the mediaeval rules of chivalry to elevate warfare for its moral worth and to make some sense of death. The Greek model of the warrior nation was held up as an example; its ideals were seen as fit for emulation; youthful heroes were to be adopted as objects of worship; and the anodyne notion that young death was swift, sweet and painless was seriously purveyed. Death lost its sting as emasculated and prettified versions of Homer provided a precedent for what was going on in South Africa and other warlike corners of the empire.[57] In 'Clifton Chapel' Newbolt praised those who learned to serve at school and later gave their lives in the fight against the Boers; Hornung preached on 'The Game of Life' as a fitting preparation for war; and in *The Hill* Vachell portrayed war as the alchemist, transmuting wayward qualities of childhood into glorious immortality via death on the battlefield.[58]

When war was declared against Germany in 1914 it was almost as if providence had given a test by which the public schools might prove their worth. War, with its call to self-sacrifice, to duty, and to honour, was seen by many as the realisation of a hope; for only in war could the hero fully realise himself, only in battle could he be put to the greatest test. The schools answered the call to arms in the most glorious of ways: young masters and senior boys set to return for the autumn term said quick farewells to their schools and volunteered almost to a man for the front. Throughout that autumn, when the war was only going to last a few months, the idealism of the public school officer was high. In this most literary of wars – with the gramophone and cinema in their infancy, and radio and television yet to come – reading became the solace, consolation, support and recreation for the educated classes; and Homer was much in demand. The Grenfell brothers, Horner, Asquith, Owen and many others read the *Odyssey* in their few leisured moments, and as the war swept towards Gallipoli so Brooke was but one to be exhilarated at the thought of reaching Homeric lands.[59] Back at home the image of 'noble and beautiful' death on the battlefield was made concrete in 'Lest We Forget' medals specially designed, and with royal approval, for families of 'Fallen Heroes'.[60] At the front the dead were often commemorated in epitaphs that echoed Simonides's monument at Thermopylae: the one above the trench on the Somme that became the tomb for 160 men of the 8th and 9th Devons recalled: 'The Devonshires held this trench. The Devonshires hold it still – yet Raymond's lines in *Tell England* are truer to the original – 'Tell England, ye who pass this monument, We died for her, and here we rest content.'[61] It is the epitaph for an heroic age.

The war that was to be the realisation of the Homeric ideal, instead witnessed its demise. Once the conflict had become bogged down in the trenches of the Western Front or on the beaches below Gallipoli, the Homeric make-believe faded away. Death had a sting: a young soldier's death was not noble and beautiful. The break was swift and clean; so too was the fall of classics. Even in the midst of war its decline was noticed: enough to prompt the prime minister, Lloyd-George, to form a committee to examine its future role in post-war Britain. The authors reported in optimistic vein; but by the time of the publication of their findings in 1921 the world had moved on: the classics had been discredited.[62]

Notes

1. Peter Parker, *The Old Lie* (London, 1987) p. 86.
2. Richard Jenkyns, *The Victorians and Ancient Greece* (Oxford, 1980) p. 61.
3. Harold Nicolson, *Good Behaviour* (London, 1955) pp. 11, 44, 51.
4. The history of British Platonism can be followed in A. E. Taylor, *Platonism and Its Influence* (London, 1925); Basil Willey, *The English Moralists* (London, 1964); and David Newsome, *Two Classes of Men* (London, 1974).
5. R. M. Ogilvie, *Latin and Greek* (London, 1964) pp. 98–101.
6. David Newsome, *Bishop Westcott and the Platonic Tradition* (Cambridge, 1969) p. 4; J. H. Buckley, *The Victorian Temper* (London, 1952/66) p. 90; Joseph E. Baker, *The Reinterpretation of Victorian Literature* (Princeton, 1950) pp. 224, 226; Frederick Maurice, *The Life of Frederick Denison Maurice* (London, 1884) ii, pp. 206-207; Mrs Charles Kingsley, *Life and Letters of Charles Kingsley* (London, 1877) ii, p. 27; E. T. Cook, *The Life of John Ruskin* (London, 1911) i, p. 354; and F. W. Cornish, *Extracts from the Letters and Journals of William Cory* (Oxford, 1897) p. 16.
7. F. A. G. Beck, *Greek Education 450–350 BC* (London, 1964) pp. 199, 239; Walter Pater, *Plato and Platonism* (London, 1893/1912) pp. 239, 241; Taylor, op. cit., pp. 58 , 60, 64, 67; Willey, op. cit., p. 42; and R. L. Nettleship, *Lectures on the Republic of Plato* (London, 1898) pp. 7–8.
8. Nicolson, op. cit., p. 54: see also R. C. Cross and A. D. Woozley, *Plato's Republic* (London, 1966) pp. 114–115; and John E. Adamson, *The Theory of Education in Plato's Republic* (London, 1903) p. 138.
9. Adamson, op. cit., pp. 46, 47, 51.
10. Thomas Arnold, *Introductory Lectures on Modern History* (London, 1842/74) p. 17.
11. Maurice, op. cit., i, pp. 30, 329; Charles E. Raven, *Christian Socialism, 1848–1854* (London, 1920) pp. 55, 56, 128; Thomas Hughes, prefatory memoir in Charles Kingsley, *Alton Locke* (London, 1876/95) p. ix; and J. F. C. Harrison, *A History of the Working Men's College* (London, 1954) p. 10.
12. Susan Chitty, *The Beast and the Monk* (London, 1974) p. 204; Guy Kendall, *Charles Kingsley and His Ideas* (London, 1947) p. 10; and Cook, op. cit., i, p. 284.
13. See, for example, David Newsome, *Godliness and Good Learning* (London, 1961) and J. B. Hope Simpson, *Rugby since Arnold* (London, 1967).
14. For a recent summary of Thring's life and work, see Malcolm Tozer, 'Education for "True Life": a Review of Thring's Educational Aims and

Methods,' *History of Education Society Bulletin*, 39 (1987). pp. 24–31; or Malcolm Tozer, 'The Great Educational Experiment: Edward Thring's Innovations at Uppingham School, 1853–1887', in Simo Seppo, *The Social Role and Evolution of the Teaching Profession in Historical Context* (Joensuu, 1988) vol. v, pp. 8–17.

15. For a summary of Thring's work in physical education, see Malcolm Tozer, 'The Joy of Strength and Movement', *Physical Education Review*, X (1987) pp. 58–63; for more details the reader should consult Malcolm Tozer, *Physical Education at Thring's Uppingham* (Uppingham, 1976).

16. For his manliness sermons, see Malcolm Tozer, 'Education in Manliness', *Religion*, XVII (1987) pp. 63-80; and Malcolm Tozer '"The Readiest Hand and the Most Open Heart": Uppingham's First Missions to the Poor', *History of Education*, XVIII (1989) pp. 323–332.

17. The most popular profession for Uppinghamians who left the school between 1853 and 1870 was the Church: see Tozer, 'Education in Manliness'.

18. *Cornhill Magazine*, May 1860, p. 611; and *Public Schools Commission* (London, 1864) i, p. 41.

19. Hughes later tried to redress the balance: see Malcolm Tozer, 'Thomas Hughes: "Tom Brown" versus "True Manliness",' *Physical Education Review*, XII (1989) pp. 44–48.

20. Herbert Spencer, *Education: Intellectual, Moral and Physical* (London, 1861/78) pp. 131–132; also see David Duncan, *The Life and Letters of Herbert Spencer* (London, 1908).

21. See J. A. Mangan, 'Athleticism: A Case Study of the Evolution of an Educational Ideology', in Brian Simon and Ian Bradley, *The Victorian Public School* (Dublin, 1975) pp. 150–152; and J. A. Mangan, *Athleticism in the Victorian and Edwardian Public School* (Cambridge, 1981) p. 99ff.

22. For the influence of Old Uppinghamians at Uppingham, see Tozer, *Physical Education at Thring's Uppingham*, pp. 137ff.

23. Various authors, *Great Public Schools* (London, 1893) pp. 171–172: see also J. R. de S. Honey, *Tom Brown's Universe* (London, 1977) chapter 4.

24. For a summary of Almond's work, see Malcolm Tozer, 'The Consecration of the Body', *Physical Education Review*, VIII (1985) p. 84ff.

25. F. W. Maitland, *The Life and Letters of Leslie Stephen* (London, 1906) pp. 61, 64, 65; Noel Annan, *Leslie Stephen* (London, 1951) p. 30; and Faith Compton Mackenzie, *William Cory* (London, 1950) pp. 40, 42.

26. Gilbert Coleridge, *Eton in the 'Seventies* (London, 1912) pp. 171, 172, 177; Percy Lubbock, *Shades of Eton* (London, 1929) p. 161; and R. H. Lyttelton, 'Eton Cricket', *National Review*, May 1894, p. 432. For more on the 'games master' see H. J. Spenser, 'The Athletic Master in Public Schools', *Contemporary Review*, July 1900, pp. 113–117.

27. C. R. L. Fletcher, *Edmund Warre* (London, 1922) pp. 27, 34, 58, 79, 92, 106.

28. J. G. Cotton Minchin, *Old Harrow Days* (London, 1898) p. 73; James Bryce, *Studies in Contemporary Biography* (London, 1903/20) pp. 350, 355; W. E. Bowen, *Edward Bowen* (London, 1902) pp. 3, 101, 115, 146, 147, 187, 225, 231; and E. E. Bowen, in Edmund W. Howson and G. T. Warner, *Harrow School* (London, 1898) p. 251.

29. E. E. Bowen (U. U.), 'Games', *Journal of Education*, 1 February 1884; William Cory, *Ionica* (London, 1905) pp. 126–128; and Annan, op. cit., p. 29.

30. B. M. G. Reardon, *From Coleridge to Gore* (London, 1971) p. 13; and Geoffrey Best, *Mid-Victorian Britain* (London, 1971) pp. 163–165.

31. This is Clement Dukes's list of the athletic virtues: Dukes was the long-serving medical officer at Rugby – *Public Schools from Within* (London, 1906) p. 183. See also J. G. Cotton Minchin, *Our Public Schools* (London, 1901) pp. 230, 231, 366.

32. Edward Lyttelton, 'Athletics in Public Schools', *Nineteenth Century*, January 1880, p. 44.

33. *Great Public Schools*, p. 179; O. F. Christie, *A History of Clifton College* (Bristol, 1935) p. 357; and Cyril Norwood, *The English Tradition of Education* (London,, 1929/31) pp. 101–105.

34. H. B. Tristram, *Loretto School* (London, 1911) p. 153; *Great Public Schools*, p. 139.

35. E. B. Castle, *Ancient Education and Today* (London, 1961/69) p. 14.

36. Ibid., p. 17.

37. Ibid., p. 14; and E. N. Gardiner, *Athletes of the Ancient World* (Oxford, 1930) p. 34.

38. Paul Fussell, *The Great War and Modern Memory* (New York, 1975) pp. 181–182.

39. Edward Lyttelton, *Memories and Hopes* (London, 1925/29) p. 43.

40. Almond also had various schemes to encourage fair play: see Tristram, op. cit., p. 122; and R. J. Mackenzie, *Almond of Loretto* (London, 1905) pp. 94, 202.

41. Christie, op. cit., p. 359.

42. Mangan, *Athleticism*, p. 68ff.

43. G. R. Parkin, *Imperial Federation* (London, 1892) pp. 7, 10, 30, 48. Parkin, a Canadian, was a frequent visitor to Uppingham, and was chosen by Thring to be his biographer: see G. R. Parkin, *Life and Letters of Edward Thring* (London, 1898). For details of Parkin's work as headmaster of Upper Canada College and Secretary of the Rhodes Scholarship scheme, see J. A. Mangan, *The Games Ethic and Imperialism* (London, 1985) pp. 149ff.

44. Charles Dilke, *The British Empire* (London, 1899) p. 1.

45. Lord Roberts was a tireless visitor to public schools: see George Forrest, *The Life of Lord Roberts* (London, 1914) p. 350.

46. W. E. Henley, *Lyra Heroica* (London, 1891); Henry Newbolt, *Collected Poems, 1897–1907* (London, 1907).

47. Rudyard Kipling, *The Five Nations* (London, 1903/48) pp. 119, 134–138.

48. Fletcher, op. cit., p. 267.

49. *Uppingham School Magazine*, February 1900, p. 1.

50. 'We hear that Mr Jones has killed five Boers single-handed. We congratulate him heartily on the exploit and hope that he will dispose of many more.' *Uppingham School Magazine*, September 1900, p. 265.

51. R. C. Rome, 'Uppingham: The Story of a School – 1584–1948', (typescript in Uppingham Archives, 1948) p. 99.

52. See, for example, the essay 'J. D. Marstock' in Harold Nicolson, *Some People* (London, 1927).
53. David Newsome, *A History of Wellington College* (London, 1959) pp. 253–257; Nicholson, *Some People*, p. 31; Arthur Ponsonby, *The Decline of the Aristocracy* (London, 1912) pp. 205–206, 241; *The Public Schools from Within*, p. 210; and Christie, op. cit., pp. 69–70.
54. Ogilvie, op. cit., p. 138; John Buchan, *Memory Hold-the-Door* (London, 1940) p. 228; and Ponsonby, op. cit., p. 249.
55. M. I. Finley, *The World of Odysseus* (London, 1964) p. 21; Beck, op. cit., p. 51; and C. M. Bowra, *Homer* (London, 1972) p. 84.
56. Castle, op. cit., pp. 12, 15; Jenkyns, op. cit., pp. 210–211; Finley, op. cit., pp. 131–133, 137; Beck, op. cit., pp. 56, 60; Ogilvie, op. cit., pp. 135–137; and Bowra, op. cit., pp. 174, 176.
57. Parker, op. cit., pp. 95, 99, 254.
58. Newbolt, op. cit., pp. 128–130; Shane R. Chichester, *E. W. Hornung and His Young Guard* (Wellington, 1941) pp. 31–37; and H. A. Vachell, *The Hill* (London, 1905) p. 303. For a recent study on Hornung, see Malcolm Tozer, 'Imperial Echoes and Ethic: E. W. Hornung and his Young Guard', in J. A. Mangan and John M. MacKenzie, *The Cultural Bond: British Imperialism and Sport* (London, 1991).
59. Parker, op. cit., pp. 217ff; and Jenkyns, op. cit., pp. 339, 342. See also Jeanne MacKenzie, *The Children of the Souls*, (London, 1986) passim.
60. Paul Fussell, *Sassoon's Longest Journey*, (New York, 1983) p. 127.
61. Parker, op. cit., p. 225; Ernest Raymond, *Tell England* (London, 1922) p. 314.
62. Ogilvie, op. cit., p. 172; and Jenkyns, op. cit., p. 345.

9

Lamentable Barbarians and Pitiful Sheep: Rhetoric of Protest and Pleasure in Late Victorian and Edwardian Oxbridge

J. A. Mangan

Hugh Kearney, in his introduction to *Scholars and Gentlemen: University and Society in Pre-Industrial Britain, 1500–1700*, described how he came slowly to the realisation that a university curriculum did not exist in a vacuum, but formed part of a wider social picture, and that universities were as much social as intellectual institutions.[1] This was, he remarked, a self-evident truth, but often hidden from view in the records of individual universities. Too often official histories were portraits without warts, resembling old-style business histories commissioned as subtle pieces of advertising. Kearney wrote of the universities before 1800; my concern is with late Victorian and Edwardian Oxford and Cambridge. Arguably, they have suffered acutely from what may be named 'Kearney's public relations syndrome'. In consequence, certain questions have preoccupied me. What was the 'Oxbridge' of the majority of students and not a few dons? Where is it recorded in any detail? Where is it discussed at any length? What were the social influences that shaped life there and how did they interact with the intellectual? What were the idealistic, utilitarian and casuistic forces at work that moulded attitudes and behaviour? What was the reality as distinct from the ideal? What was the common as distinct from the uncommon atmosphere? Was there anything approaching a predominant ethos that governed the lives and determined the lifestyles of many, if not most undergraduates and some dons? What is missing from encomiums such as T. B.

Howarth's 'evidence' in support of J. B. Priestley's assertion regarding the Cambridge 'lost generation' of the Great War, that nothing would distract him from the belief, which he would take to the grave, that the generation to whom he belonged, destroyed between 1914 and 1918, was a great generation, marvellous in its promise. Howarth wrote:

As an example, Geoffrey Hopley of Trinity went down in 1914, by which time he had secured a double first in the History Tripos, passed all his Bar examinations in one year, won a cricket blue and a heavy-weight boxing blue. He died of septicaemia after being shot by a sniper. In the very last months of the war Geoffrey Tatham, Fellow and Junior Bursar of Trinity and already a historian of distinction was killed as a mere captain, aged thirty-four. James Woolston of Pembroke, a Professor of Mathematics in South Africa, died of wounds as a lance corporal. D. H. L. Baynes of Clare with a first in Mathematics and another in Natural Sciences was killed age thirty-two; Allan Parke of Jesus was killed just over a month before the Armistice, having been wounded at Suvla Bay in 1915 and twice in France on the same day in 1917; Philip Bainbridge, killed in September 1918 as a Second Lieutenant, had won a first in both parts of the Classical Tripos; Donald Innes, a Classical Exhibitioner at Trinity, went to the front as a Second Lieutenant in the Black Watch in August 1918 and died of wounds aged nineteen on 6 October; of Jesus College's 150 war casualties one, Francis Storrs, was killed on 10 November, the last day of the war.[2]

Eight tragic heroes. The substance of a generation?

Between approximately 1875 and 1914 there was a new and heady fashion abroad in the 'ancient universities'. River and games field had moved close to the centre of collegiate life.[3] These elements are not to be dismissed as insignificant to the history of these famous institutions. To begin with, they changed the topography of both towns. And in this regard they stood as symbols of the period values of an upper middle class educational system and culture. They represented contradictory and powerful social forces: moral idealism, class conspicuous consumption, sensible utilitarianism, circumscribed hedonism, class insulation, unconscious and defiant quixotry. Furthermore, they constituted, as I have written elsewhere, load-bearing supports underpinning the moral, educational and social structures of British and Imperial society.[4] For too long their significance has been insensitively neglected.

Writing retrospectively, in 1921, of college athletics clubs within the university, W. W. Rouse Ball, Fellow of Trinity College, Cambridge, observed that 'growth of organised recreations of this kind will strike the future historian as one of the outstanding features of the last century.'[5] Ball did not equivocate. He thrust directly to the heart of the matter. For this reason: he had lived through the days of this rampant ethos. He had both witnessed and experienced it at first hand. He knew both its potency and its pervasiveness. He also had some conception of its cultural significance. A few years before Rouse Ball, the famous W. H. Spooner, Fellow and eventually Warden of New College, Oxford, in his unpublished memoirs, 'Fifty Years in an Oxford College', wrote that 'The university pulpit was still in the years 1862–67 [the years when he was an undergraduate at New College] a great power in the university,' and he continued,

> The decay in interest in sermons, of which we hear so much, is partly a fashion. In some measure, it is the result of a more extended interest in history and science, and *above all in games* [emphasis added] . . .which has been among the most marked effects of our popular education.[6]

It was his view that in the 1860s the university had probably reached a high-water mark of intellectual activity and preeminence. Since then, it had been all dispersion. His generation had not been 'under the tyranny of athleticism'. In his view later generations were. It is not difficult to sweep a dragnet through the literary shoals of period biographies, memoirs, reminiscences and commentaries and add them to the Ball/Spooner catch. There is the acidic editorial in the *Cambridge Review* of 23 November 1893 on classical education in Cambridge: 'Matthew Arnold once said of the English aristocracy, "They hunt, they shoot, they fish, but they do not think." Not without some justification might an analogous criticism be passed on the Cambridge classical man.'[7] There is the *Spectator*'s attack in May 1886 on 'frantic athleticism' in the universities:

> It is a curious fact that just at the time when we are all endeavouring to educate our masters, as the late Lord Sherbert put it,

the great feature of the higher education, should be a very well marked revolt of the body against the mind, of athleticism against the predominance of the intellect or even the finer tastes. Talk to any great university teachers of the day, and they will tell you there is no longer the same passionate interest in the higher studies which there was fifty years ago . . . What really stirs enthusiasm in the youthful mind at the present moment is the education of the body . . . All the higher ambition of the university is ambition to succeed in the achievements which should be at best *amusements*. We look with some alarm on the steady decline of the higher intellectual interests in our Universities. There is no teacher past middle age who does not see how much the ardour of intellectual investigation has fallen off since he first began to teach. Our great schools and universities are no longer the nurseries of the acutest minds of the country, they are nurseries of the most agile bodies . . .[8]

There is the jaundiced and pointed comment in the form of a generalised *Valete* in *Granta* of 5 March 1898: 'Looking back, what do we recognize? The memory of a few faceless friendships, a faint echo of excessive physical exercise and the doubtful acquisition of knowledge!'[9] And there are rueful comments of a disillusioned Anglophile, Haji Kirmanshahi, in the same magazine four years later. On first acquaintance, he had hailed with joy, he said, youths with a bloom on their faces sauntering in the sun. Here was the rising hope of England. He stood in respect of their manly sports and their intellectual disciplines, and praised the system that trained at once the body and the mind. Closer inspection of the reality, however, tempered his enthusiasm. Here and there, he later related sadly, he had met a man interested in research. Such men there were, but how few. How few among the young, how fewer still among the old. A sadder and wiser man, he had discovered that there were men at Cambridge who openly expressed their contempt for all forms of study, others who conceived of a college as a club. And it was these men who controlled the destiny of the university, depressed its spirit, and in a Freudian metaphor he added, bound it with magic cords in the net of an unfruitful tradition. He called on Bacon, Milton, Newton and Darwin to serve as sources of necessary regeneration.[10]

A startled Rhodes scholar from Germany noted in the *Cornhill Magazine* of 1905 that one of the most important factors of English student life was the cult of athletics.[11] In consequence, he assigned absolute supremacy in athletics to the English universities, but claimed the lead in the pursuit of knowledge for the Germans. He was frankly astounded at the ignorance of the young Englishman and the paucity of his knowledge of history, geography, and the literature of his own language. But without irony and with Teutonic sobriety, he generously exonerated him from blame by pointing out that he had so little time for pursuing his scholarly education, with his drawn-out breakfasts (sometimes two hours), his subsequent conscientious common-room perusal of the *Sporting Chronicle*, and the climax of his day: the afternoon's strenuous strife on the green turf. 'Magister Regens', for his part, writing on the reform of Oxford and Cambridge in the *Oxford and Cambridge Review* of July 1911, argued the pressing need for a university commission, adding, 'If it were a very wise tribunal indeed, it might be able, while conserving the legitimate interests of manly sport, to do just a little towards solving the crucial problem of excessive athletics.'[12]

In such an atmosphere, it was certainly not fortuitous that *Granta*, in mild fun admittedly, announced in February 1905 that, to celebrate the first professorship in football at the university, an inaugural lecture would be delivered by Bill Bailey, Demonstrator in Football to the university and Corresponding Member to the Football Institute of Tokyo. It further added that Paley's *Evidences* had been replaced by Sandow's *Evidences of Health* and that the English race had at last been emancipated from the dominion of the intellect.[13] *Isis* for its part, rather more seriously, in February 1895 argued for appropriate degrees for athletes, claiming with some truth that the oarsmen from Eton, the cricketers from Harrow or Winchester, the footballers from Charterhouse, Clifton, Loretto and Sherborne had made Oxford what she was, and that the miserable pittance of a Pass Degree was out of all proportion to the merits of its recipients.[14]

Late Victorian and Edwardian Oxford and Cambridge, while differing in some regards, were strikingly similar not merely in accordance with *Granta*'s observation, 'The cut of our clothes, the manner of our speech are much the same as those affected by Oxford men, away then with imaginary differences, strike an average all round, the result would be the same in either case,'[15] but in one further highly significant regard – the lifestyles of the undergraduates. 'It cannot be denied', remarked Frank Rutter in his *Varsity Types: Scenes and Characters from Undergraduate Life*, published in 1911, ' that the visitor to Oxford and Cambridge is often impressed with the idea that recreation and amusement form the real work here, and that study is merely useful insofar as it goes to fill up some corner of the day's routine, which cannot be otherwise allocated.'[16] Rowland Prothero once wrote, 'Life in the universities has been too exclusively described in the autobiographies of men whose subsequent careers were only the fruit of their brilliant triumphs of school and college. As in boyhood and youth, they belonged to that distinguished minority who made the fullest use of their educational opportunities.'[17] This is a quotation to ponder, to linger over, and to remember. It hints at a widely unrecognised reality. Oxbridge between 1875 and 1914, was more a place of privileged play than it was a centre of meritocratic cerebral effort. To fashion a simile, it was like a bottle of milk which, far from being heavy with rich cream, was in fact of very moderate quality, with only a thin creamy layer at the rim and a considerable quantity of watery residue.

The 'ancient universities', of the late nineteenth century, were finishing schools for public schoolboys.[18] These ebullient and hearty members of the *jeunesse dorée* were thick upon the ground. Their influence was all-pervasive. The *Gownsman* of 6 May 1911 contained a rueful letter from the son of a poor but educated man who had been at a newer university college. 'Poverty', he remarked, 'was not a virtue at Cambridge. The association with the public-school atmosphere is so persistent that individuals from unknown schools . . . would not succeed in getting the best from Cambridge as Cambridge would scarce feel their influence.'[19] Both universities were open and defiant bastions of privilege, but energetic, not lethargic, privilege. For the majority, muscle grew there, if not intellect. *Granta* recorded of E. W. Lord of Trinity Hall in May 1891, for example, that he soon discovered that rowing was more important than reading and that the instruction received in the former was greatly superior to that of the latter and, furthermore, there was no comparison between the two types of coach. Lord, therefore, set his mind on muscular development.[20] In short, the public pleasures of many of the undergraduates were robust. The desirable attainments of manhood were epitomised for many by J. H. D. Willoughby, President of the Athenaeum Club in 1889, and singled out for attention in *Granta*'s weekly celebrity spot 'Those in Authority' in February of the same year: 'He plays fives.

He holds office in the Trinity cricket club and stags fall by the thousand to his rifle . . . He used to run with the beagles at Eton and still goes the pace. Having formerly been Keeper of the Field, he is now an Eton Rambler.'[21] Willoughby was typical of literally hundreds of 'heroes' celebrated in 'Those in Authority', and its equivalent, '*Isis* Idols', of the Oxford student magazine, the *Isis*, during the years before the Great War.[22] The fact of the matter was that the compelling ideology of athleticism had captured the public school system, and its strongly indoctrinated products moved *en masse* into the ancient universities and shaped them in their image.

The ideology was never as dominant in the universities as it was in the schools, and it varied in intensity from college to college and from period to period, but it became woven tightly into the social and educational fabric of college life. It dictated attitudes and actions. It has never been set in institutional context, and its influence has never received the attention that it merits in part, no doubt, because it is now perceived, to hark back to Kearney, as a wart rather than a beauty spot. It was perceived very differently a hundred years ago.

In this chapter we are mostly concerned with one manifestation of student commitment – the literature of ideological allegiance. I throws new light on the frequently sour relations between dons and undergraduates which existed well beyond the period of *The Revolution of the Dons*.[23] The rhetoric of both student pleasure and protest reveals continuing and widespread hostility between many college staff and most of their charges as public school fashion swept the universities in the second half of the nineteenth century. This antagonism was reduced only by the active support for the new student enthusiasms by those dons who adjusted to the fresh imperatives and who became a Profane Leadership endorsing the now prevailing ideology. Their part in promoting both institutional accord and ideological change merits, and therefore will also receive, consideration.

For much of the late nineteenth and early twentieth centuries Brasenose College, Oxford was noted for its record of outstanding success on river and field, its hearty, uncomplicated 'chaps', and an early obsessive philathletic Principal, E. H. Craddock.[24] It was a tradition widely endorsed. On the occasion of his successor, Charles Willer Heberden, becoming Principal in 1889, *Grant* stretched out a hand of friendship to the other university and expressed the hope that the muscle of the athletes would still hol its own against the heads of the bookworms in good old Brasenose.[25] In fact, things were changing slightly, and in the *Oxford and Cambridge Review* of July 1911, F. W. Bussell, Vice Principal of Brasenose, indicated as much in a defiant gesture of exasperated defensiveness.[26] He defended with blunt vigour what he called, 'The Old System of Education.' He presented it as a still centre in a whirling hurricane of ill-conceived change. Irritated by the endless criticism of the ancient universities, the frenzied proposals for reform and the pusillanimity of the Old Guard, he offered an apologia for the aristocratic concept of university education. He traced its development from the democratic ideal of the medieval church, which sought ability chiefly among the poor, to the conservative function of the later Oxford of the Hanoverian era. The university, once the home of free thought, had by then become an instrument of central government, and trained men marked out by birth for office and the business and burdens of social life. As such, he argued, the university was neither competitive nor utilitarian. It promised neither social advancement nor profit. It prepared for careers already certain. This inherited and long tradition at Oxford was now assaulted. And the assault was presumptuous. What, after all, was the end of education? Was it selfish and personal, or public and disinterested? The labourer might exchange his corduroy for the clerk's black coat, the call might go out to seek the universities and the posts and pensions that would follow, the talk might be of civic duty and social service; the practice, however, was individualistic and competitive. In a sentence, modern education was founded on self-interest. In consequence, it was seen as monstrous that the university should be the private hunting ground of the privileged. Such resentment, he stated, was ill founded. The education of public school and university was aristocratic in the truest sense. In a phrase, *noblesse oblige*. Public school and university were the twin instruments of this upper class imperative. At school, the silent training, the routine of command and the 'curious gravity of recreation' (a telling expression) created the independent, alert, self-reliant Englishman. This training continued successfully in the ancient universities. There were differences: more solitary work, more individualism, yet 'the Commonwealth' stood in first place. The sense of the college drove away base and greedy thoughts of mere personal advancement. The holy ground protected by monastic taboos was separated not only from the world but from the university. The college was the source of 'an elective system of useful self-government: athletics and the corporate life'. Patriotism was displayed in acts not essays (a splendid aphorism). Yet this self-evident virtue was under threat. Aristocratic control was losing ground to the Tchinovik. *Noblesse oblige* was going out of fashion, and with it its system of training. There was a new theory abroad. Intellect, not character, was to rule the world. Was it not possible however, asked Bussell, that intellect might not imply character? Some happily still acknowledged this. A rear-guard action was still being fought. Thankfully there was opposition still to tests of mere ability. Almost everywhere there was an attempt to go beyond the results of mere competitive success. The teacher, the ruler, the civilian for subject races, were chosen for qualities other than cleverness. The reality could not be denied. Public school and university had produced character *apart* from book learning, and character was what counted. Consequently more time was wasted in lectures than at games.

Up to this point, Bussell's arguments had tumbled out with tempestuous passion. He regained composure and added reflectively, and it was just as well, that, of course, all was not perfect in an imperfect world, the aristocratic ideal was seldom seen in its purity, and had sometimes sunk into woeful caricature. But it still beckoned. He fired his Parthian shot – so long as character was valued above aptitude, so long would the schools and colleges flourish.

The fissures in the foundations of his argument were wide. And in addition, he ruined whatever case he had by prejudice, snobbishness and hysteria. But he *made* it. And this is his value to the historian. His conservatism shone like a blazing beacon on a bare hill. And, as he declared, what he had stated many in the universities thought. He stood as a guardian at the gates defending corporate and corporeal college values. In this posture of defiance, I suggest, he caught exactly the collegiate ethos of the times. In conjunction with the Oxbridge of exhibitioners and scholars, research degrees, professional scholarship and university professorships there existed a larger Oxbridge of philistine public schoolboys, and enthusiastic, committed, acquiescent or calculating dons, frequently, of course, from the same schools, and increasingly as the nineteenth century closes on the twentieth, products of the same ideological process. And these types are not to be confused with the later Brideshead brigade. They looked with distaste on the Sebastian Flytes. Their values were far more muscular. And there is a further point of great importance. It is not commonly appreciated that the Oxbridge collegiate system was a glorified house system – the very instrument of social engineering that so effectively sustained the ideology of athleticism in the public schools.

In the 1896 tercentenary edition of the *Pheon*, the magazine of Sydney Sussex College, G. M. Edwards, Fellow and Tutor of the College, made cutting reference to the phenomenal growth of athleticism during the previous twenty years.[27] The pursuit of the ideal *mens sana in corpore sano*, he remarked, had produced not a *mens sana*, but a *corpus vile* in which King Nous did not sit upon the throne, yet Edwards admitted that if athletics did one good thing, it furnished a theme for healthy and apparently inexhaustible conversation.

This fashion exasperated not only Edwards, but many of the dons. It posed serious problems. The new breed of public schoolboy entering the universities indulged themselves as fulsomely and as energetically as earlier students, but had new pastimes, caught perfectly in this trite pastiche, 'Tea Time: An Elegy' from the *Griffin*, the magazine of Downing College, Cambridge:

> The R. C. chimes the hour of closing day,
> The hockey team winds slowly home to tea,
> The oarsman homeward plods his weary way,
> And leaves the quad to darkness and to me.[28]

As well as taking up rowing they inhabited games fields in large numbers as colleges responded to their public school derived needs and demands. These boys now hit and kicked balls on fields rather than riding horse-races on turnpikes. And as a direct result relationships between them and the dons were frequently strained: a sorry state of affairs that was revealed in a mocking little verse, 'The Plaint of the Ancient Don', which appeared in the *Lady Clare* Magazine of 1898:

> Through the streets and colleges I repair,
> The students banter and fist at me
> Or make remarks as they rudely stare;
> They call me, I think, 'the primeval he'.[29]

E. C. M., indulging in some random reminiscences of Lincoln College, Oxford at the turn of the century, remembered that relations between dons and undergraduates were sour, the former being regarded by the latter as their natural enemies.[30] *Granta*, a little earlier, had written on the subject of staff and students at Cambridge in precisely the same terms: 'Few people would be so bold as to deny that the present relationship between don and undergraduate is in many regards singularly unsatisfactory; that there still exists a large class of men who look upon dons as their natural enemies.'[31] Between many dons and most undergraduates there was now more than a generational gap, there was a new and yawning ideological one. The student image of the don, an image sharpened by new and extended pleasures, was often that of a decrepit killjoy, 'A fossil bodied in a chalky soil, and fit for nothing, save for crabbed toil', as an unpleasant little distiche of the time had it.[32] 'What is it to be a don?', asked another unmerciful undergraduate versifier,

> It is to know at length
> The pedant's rich reward in blinded eyes,
> And fading strength,
> A palsied heart too dull to sympathise
> With human joys?
> A head that aches at every slightest noise,
> And – worse beyond all question –
> Constant indigestion.[33]

He was, in effect, 'the don without a past' – the title of a verse in *Granta* of January 1897.

> When I look at adolescence
> In its garb of vernal green
> Bitter thoughts of wasted pleasance
> Rise from out the Might have been;
> Wake a fond regret concerning
> Balmy Manhood's budding time
> Set my feeble gizzard yearning
> For my undergraduate prime.
>
> Though my rather manly figure
> Turned the scale at 13.2,
> I declined with steady vigour

Every blessed sort of blue;
What was muscular repute, or
Skill in potting of the white
'Dust and ashes,' said my tutor,
And I fancied he was right.[34]

In short, the dull don denied life. As a disgruntled student cried plaintively in the *Oxford Magazine* of 1905:

I sit and write of what I hear him drone
Of Roman senates and worn-out states,
But my soul to a far-off place is flown,
Where minds are lusty, and all the gates
Of life stand wide with a beckoning gleam.[35]

And a heart-rending cry in similar vein appeared in the *Cambridge Review* about the same time.

A lecture room in the middle of spring
Is a god-forsaken and desolate thing
When winds are blowing on Maddingley Hill
And waters are flowing at Trumpington Mill.

Oh, what can it matter at all?
Oh, what can it matter to me?
That Caesar conquered Gaul
In 58 BC?[36]

The wheel of student retribution sped faster as the 1890s progressed. Both *Granta* and *Isis* were increasingly and determinedly cruel at the expense of the dons. A *Granta* editorial of 1896 on 'Dons and their Uses' explored their origins and evolution in malicious terms.[37] They were, it stated, frousy old men with matted grey beards. Certainly men of deep learning and impeccable orthodoxy, but established originally by whim of king or wealthy gentleman due to the sting of conscience, after a misspent life. And now, self-appointed, they constituted bodies which selected those of the same propensities and of the same eventual appearance, yet, while they were unchanging, the young men in their charge had greatly changed: no longer scholars but men sent to Cambridge to receive a final polish before going out into the world. The outcome was a society of undergraduates presided over by men, very few of whom had anything in common with the younger members of their college. It did not seem right, the editorial concluded, that social and physical qualifications should be denied in favour of an abnormally developed brain power: 'Why should a man who possesses all the attributes of a gentleman be passed in the race by a person who esteems Madvig's syntax more highly than his morning bath?' That same year, *Granta* chose as its university type for analysis 'The Mere Don' – met with, it declared, in all colleges in fairly large numbers.[38] Therefore a not uncommon species. Having gained its fellowship, *Granta* observed unpleasantly, the rest of its career was simply a question of the degree of social and spiritual nonentity which it would attain. Sterility soon settled all the intellect. To lecture in a merely donnish way was soon learned – the subject being divested of any possible interest. As the instrument for the advancement of knowledge, the don was a complete and lamentable failure. And the same dismal fact had to be reported in regard to the other half of his duty: the undergraduate of his college. The don was wholly ignorant of his state of being. The most serious charge of all that the magazine levelled at the unfortunate scholar, however, was his inclination to marry a mere donnish wife and produce more of his own kind! *Isis* was no less unpleasant in a sharp little foray against the dons in March 1899. Subsequent to the intervention of the Parliamentary Commission of recent years, a most artful process of selecting Fellows had been designed. Book-readers were preferred to those with active knowledge of life. *Isis* considered that now more than ever it would be fit and proper if Fellows were chosen who were gentlemen and had some familiarity with undergraduates.[39]

Complaints of lack of sympathy with the undergraduate, especially his enthusiasm for field and river, was commonplace in the pages of the student magazines.

> Who for me doesn't care a pin
> But notwithstanding, thinks no sin
> To rake my golden shekels in?
> My tutor.
>
> Who studied all his youthful days?
> And won the prizes in the Mays
> And cannot understand my ways?
> My tutor.[40]

An open letter to a don in *Granta* of January, 1898 reads: 'You exhibit no sympathy with us, no interest in our somewhat limited universe . . . you contemplate us as a set of lamentable barbarians; we regard you as a species of pitiful sheep.'[41] In these years, the undergraduate wail of bitterness was loud against 'that faded world of weak bodies and spent minds, that half life passed in accumulating knowledge which would be of no use to others'.[42] Arcane prejudice in favour of book learning, claimed an editorial in the *Silver Crescent* the magazine of Trinity Hall, Cambridge, in 1901, 'was destroying the collegiate spirit'. Sportsmen were urged to ignore the learned don in the mean role of Volpine Machiavelli, to be deaf to his silken tones as he enlarged upon the blessedness of bookworming or in a more bitter mood as he anathematized the body. Anticipating Bussell by some ten years, the authors argued that the traditions of the Hall could only be upheld by working hard at play. Resist, they urged, all that would be a lure from the fellowship of the temples of field and lawn.[43]

Occasionally the satirist used verse as the medium of sardonic exhortation, and so served, albeit sarcastically, to underline common attitudes and aspiration.

> Let dons delight their books to write,
> Who nothing else can do;
> Let bookworms keep the lamps alight,
> For 'tis their nature to.

> But undergrads should never let
> Such foolish customs rise;
> You came not to the 'Varsity
> To blear and spoil your eyes.

> How different the early years
> Of some immortal blue!
> The daring feats he used to try,
> The little that he knew!

> His soul was always high and bold
> And as he grew in size,
> He grew more muscular and strong,
> If not more learned and wise.

> His brain was empty as a pan
> But ah, he learned to row;
> What matter if the god-like man
> Was ploughed in "Little Go"?
>
> In outdoor games and healthful play
> Let your three years be passed,
> That you may give of every day
> A good account at last.[44]

The first lines of a sarcastic little verse in the *Oxford Magazine* of
November 1890, inspired by the bold and wholly sincere statement
from Lord Roseberry, to the effect that nothing afforded such
lessons for national success as association football, went:

> If you ask for the cause of our national flaws,
>   and the reason we are blamed for our vices. . .
> We are too much controlled by academies old
>   on the banks of the Cam and the Isis;
>
> 'Tis the methods of cram by the Isis and Cam
>   that provide an excuse for the mocker,
> With the languages dead that they put in your head,
>   with their rooted aversion for soccer.

While the last verse was an admonition without any doubt taken
seriously by many:

> Then behave as you're told, oh academies old
>   and reform all your ancient foundations
> And reflect (as I've shown) that athletics alone
>   are a way to regenerate nations:
>
> For whatever the blows we receive from our foes
>   we've a shot that remains in the locker,
> And our efforts success will assuredly bless
>   if we only are faithful to soccer.[45]

An equally sardonic correspondent in *Granta* in 1891 had tried to
avoid just such a crisis of national confidence as illustrated in the
lines above when he contributed to some lengthy correspondence

on the subject of 'Are dons a failure?' with a suggestion that a mission be set up for dons, with courses in football, cricket, rugby, and rowing, supervised by captains of the various teams of the colleges.[46]

In 1885 the *Oxford Review*, written by undergraduates for undergraduates, in an article on Mark Pattison, presented an interesting view of that great reforming Fellow of Lincoln College. It had nothing good to say. 'From the general mass of the college', the writer observed, 'he held himself almost completely aloof. He showed no interest in rowing, football or any of the athletics, which formed such an invaluable part of an Oxford education. This was undoubtedly a great misfortune.'[47] And the author of the piece added, for good measure, that 'the whole tendency of college life was to draw strong lines of demarcation between don and undergraduate, a bad arrangement for both. The latter are reduced to schoolboys; the former are isolated to an extent unknown in any reputable school.'[48] The *Lady Clare Magazine* about this time sent a flight of sharp satirical arrows in the direction of the dons. They sped along the curve and flight of a narrow and wholly predictable trajectory. In a batch of fictitious leaves from a tutor's diaries, one page read:

Lectured at nine . . . or rather, was in the lecture room at nine, and found it empty. At 9.15 half the class arrived, very sleepy and cross . . . Spent the rest of the morning correcting compositions. Astonishing what indifference my pupils show to the feelings of ancients . . . Smith . . . although I am told he is Captain of the Boat Club, seems unable to grasp the principle of 'diek plus'! Says they don't do it in the Mays . . .wouldn't be sporting.[49]

That there was more than a ring of truth to this pitiful ejaculation is demonstrated in an editorial in the *Griffin*, which proclaimed early in 1905 that the New Year had produced the usual good resolutions and 'The authorities will be pleased to hear that one second year man, to our certain knowledge, is regularly attending nine o'clock lectures; with the optimism common to editors we believe that, despite training breakfasts, a diligent search might disclose another.'[50]

A page from another don's equally fictitious diary in the *Lady Clare Magazine* complained of a large crowd watching a football match as he rode home on his bicycle; an enthusiasm beyond his comprehension and invariably followed by expensive dinners and breaches of discipline, particularly when champagne was 'partaken of'.[51] As late as 1907 the magazine contained a 'complaint' from an anonymous don, demanding why he failed to win student respect.

> Horace's *mens sana in corpore sano* is the *via media* to which most men aspire, I'm higher. I yearn to see the physical desires entirely subordinated to the mind. I take the *summum bonum* of life to be *scientia*, and therefore reject all mundane pleasures. Like all great men, I pay the strictest attention to detail, after spending hour upon hour upon *varias lectiones* such as 'si' and 'se' in a doubtful text. Yet in spite of all of my learning, I seldom meet with the respect due to my genius, especially from the undergraduate body.[52]

The editors, who had probably written the letter in the first place, replied: 'You are an intellectual snob, sir. You strive all your life against nature. You have a body. What right have you to suppress it? Don't you realise you are human like the rest of us . . .?'[53] In the face of such student contumely, and with the clearest indication from them as to what constituted an acceptable member of the college, is it so improbable that Richard Bird wrote *The Laggard in Love: An Improbable Comedy* in 1911, in which the plot concerned the youthful Junior Dean of St Chad's who, after several delectable days in the Backs during May week with a young lady visitor, proposed marriage, only to receive a most delicate hint that, had he been a Blue, she would have looked on him more favourably. He immediately resigned from St Chad's, went as an undergraduate to Selby, and became a strong candidate for a place in the university XV.[54]

There is, of course, the most serious point in this satire, parody, and doggerel. Deep antagonism between many dons and most students, the result of their different perceptions of college and university life, could only be mitigated or dissipated by the action of the dons themselves. For the most part, those who won admiration, respect and affection from their public school charges, unsurprisingly shared their physical enthusiasms. Such men were spread widely throughout the colleges of the universities, and existed at every level. Collectively, they formed a Profane Leadership which embraced the values of Bussell as much as, or sometimes in preference to, those of Pattison. Some certainly cocked a snook at the sacred orthodoxy of intellectualism, and established themselves as a rival group of sacerdotalists.

'One of the peculiarities of the English intellectual *qua* gentleman', argues Gertrude Himmelfarb, 'is the survivor of the schoolboy in him,' and later in the same essay on 'Leslie Stephen: The Victorian Intellectual', she remarks: 'There is no other country where both the wit of sportsmanship and the physical activity of sport have penetrated so deeply into society as to determine the character of its intellectuals.'[55] On sports, she claims, Stephen, like most of his countrymen, 'lavished a passionate enthusiasm which they withheld from most other activities, especially religion. Sports could be indulged to excess as nothing else could, and they acquired a respect that nothing else did. Perfect in themselves, they provided a model for all else.'[56] These are shrewd observations. And they apply, of course, as much to a good number of Oxbridge dons of late Victorian and Edwardian England as fittingly as they apply to Stephen. Many of these men, like Stephen, again to echo Himmelfarb, were as intellectual as their compulsive sense of manliness permitted them. And manliness drove a hard bargain. Wardens, presidents, provosts, masters and rectors of Oxbridge colleges played their part as self-appointed institutional sachems, endorsing an 'unholy' movement within the universities in the second half of the nineteenth century and later. They sometimes had considerable power, and in some cases, such as Craddock and Stallybrass at Brasenose, Oxford, Morgan at Jesus, and Rushmore at St Catherine's, Cambridge, they could, and did, fill their colleges with young gentlemen of the right type – more athletic than academic. The role that the Oxbridge college titans adopted appears to be self-assigned. And, as self-appointed leaders of unsanctified fashion, they need to be rescued from obscurity if the potency of this fashion is to be fully gauged.

One of the earliest and warmest supporters of the active undergraduate was Ben Latham, 'best loved of the *custodes* of Trinity Hall, Cambridge',[57] as its magazine once proclaimed. Latham was born at Dover in 1821. He was considered insufficiently sturdy for a public school education. As the *Cambridge Review* suggested in 1902 he had neither the strength nor the inclination for boys' games, but was a great and general reader.[58] In later life he possibly read less and certainly rowed more. (He was a member of the Cambridge 'Ancient Mariners', an enthusiastic group of rowing dons, until he was over 70.) He entered Trinity College in 1841 and graduated as eighteenth Wrangler in 1845. His career as a student appears to be unexceptional, except for a stubborn insistence on eating cauliflowers while in training for the second Trinity boat. In 1847 he was appointed Tutor of Trinity Hall, became Senior Tutor in 1855 and Master in 1888. From 1847 to 1888 he was 'the mainspring of the college, the ideal of what a college Tutor should be.'[59] He was no mere titular guardian, but one who was keenly interested in the students' welfare, and knew how to promote it. The image of the don as 'some sort of clerical old woman' simply did not fit. Here was a man of presence: 'big, downright worldly wise'.[60] He remained unmarried, and in a real sense his boys were his family; and, as such, he won their affection and respect. Throughout the years of both his direct and indirect leadership at Trinity, his special interest was the poll man – the ordinary as distinct from the honours undergraduate – far more numerous and far less academic. He had more time for the honest, clean-minded boy who did his best than for the clever boy who gave himself airs. And if the plodding trier was keen on the boats, so much the better. Latham's commonsensical, down-to-earth philosophy comes through strongly in the sermon he preached in the chapel of Trinity Hall following the funeral of the Reverend Thomas Markby, Classical Lecturer at the Hall until 1870.[61]

Of Markby he said (and he could well have been speaking of himself) that he could not bear intellectual cockscombry. With such arrogance he had little patience. Latham, for his part, understood that human beings were not merely vessels to hold intellect, and further he recognised that those less likely to gain education from books should seek education of the active life on the river instead. Many of his students needed no second bidding. With such views Latham undoubtedly set a tone for the Hall. And he knew what he was about. He was a realist. He valued the boats 'chiefly as a means of self-disciplining the men'.[62] He wanted to maintain numbers (in an insignificant hall) *and* maintain discipline. No easy matter to combine the two. In short, for him, sport in the Hall was a sound system of control. But there was more to it than this. He held firmly to the view that a university education was more a training in character than in intellect. Significantly, therefore, he preferred wide involvement on the river rather than winning teams. And in his mind the river was an integral part of university life. Rowing was not an extracurricular recreation, but a central component of the collegiate curriculum. Latham was very much a man of his time in his suspicion of the clever and his support of the decent and the strenuous. The ethos of Trinity under his guardianship represented that of a well-run period public school under a hearty, benevolent, no-nonsense headmaster.

To balance Cambridge with Oxford enthusiasm we will return briefly to Brasenose and consider W. T. S. Stallybrass, Fellow in 1911, Vice Principal in 1924 and Principal in 1936. 'Rarely has an institution', wrote a former member of the college, 'been so completely identified with one man.'[63] It was his policy, stated the same writer, to fill the college with men of character. Among the ingredients of character, as he defined it, athletic ability took a high place, consequently the college's success in every form of sport was remarkable. Its critics thought it was too remarkable. Brasenose was known as a great athletic institution. Stallybrass's preoccupation with games ensured wide contact with public school masters who pushed their promising athletes in his direction. For many years Brasenose was the foremost Oxford college for 'hearties', and in this respect was the equivalent of Jesus at Cambridge. Stallybrass was not the exception at Brasenose. Others had established and obtained an athletocracy well before him. The Reverend Edward Hartopp Craddock, Principal from 1853 to 1886, whom we have already met and who, as we have seen, was noted for his admiration of the athlete, and his Vice Principal, Bussell, whom we have also met earlier, both gave the athletic ethos their strong support. What must not be overlooked is that such men in positions of authority had a long and significant influence on college priorities and on undergraduate membership. Some idea of the tone of the college throughout the second half of the nineteenth century can be gleaned from the recollections of Brian Jones, looking back to mid-century Brasenose: 'I don't know what Brasenose is now, but in my day it was not a reading college. Many of the undergraduates were the sons of Cheshire squires, and if there had been honours obtained for knowledge of the science of fox hunting, they would have done extremely well.'[64] Craddock, it is recorded, saw Douglas Haig (later Field Marshal) crossing the Brasenose lawn in his hunting outfit in the 1880's, and called out to him: 'Ride, sir, ride! I like to see the gentlemen of Brasenose in top boots.'[65] And it was Bussell, clearly on the side of the geneticists rather than the environmentalists on this occasion, who stated at a college dinner after a lean year on the river that it was the duty of old Brasenose men to see the right type of fellow continue to come to the college. And if they did their duty, matrimonially it seems to be implied, the college would preserve its traditions.

The last of the Profane Leadership to be considered in this brief review is Charles Taylor, Fellow of St John's College, Cambridge from 1864 to 1881 and Master from 1881 to 1888. Taylor was neither a mere bookworm nor a cloistered recluse. In the Cambridge fashion of the time, he was a good walker, an honest horseman, and an indefatigable mountaineer. He is mentioned here because in a Prize Day speech he gave in 1901 to the pupils of the Royal Grammar School, Lancaster, he provided a glimpse of a philosophy of education that throws light not only on him but on the college he served and on the Cambridge of his time.

> . . .learning is not the whole of education. It is a vulgar error that a boy goes to school merely to learn a number of things that may be useful to him. The aim of a grammar school is not to prepare a boy for a particular trade or profession, but to train him in character and mind and physically, so that he may be able to live the highest possible life in whatever position he may be placed.[66]

However it is Taylor's rider that is most revealing:

> A point which I must not leave unnoticed is the importance of good games, not only for bodily training, but as a contribution to the formation of character. It is remarkable how high a standard of morality is insisted upon by boys and men in athletic exercises. When in matters of life and death we say, 'Let there be fair play,' we take for granted that everyone expects truth and fairness in play. In small things and great in schoolwork and in the later battle of life, resolve and endeavour to live up to the moral standard of your play.[67]

Here is an Oxbridge educator of his era. Like Latham, Craddock, Stallybrass and a number of other college heads, Taylor had a concept of education indistinguishable from that of the late Victorian public school headmaster.

In his *Republic*, Plato advocated as rulers of the state a class of guardians – those of the standing army of the strong, the swift, the brave and high spirited and the gentle, with, of course, a taste for philosophy. From this superior class were to be chosen the magistrates – the oldest, most prudent, most wise, most patriotic and most unselfish members of the society. These were called the True Guardians. The remainder were called Auxiliaries. The True Guardians were philosophers, with such characteristics as a desire for knowledge, a love of truth, contempt for the pleasures of the body, open-mindedness, indifference to money, quick understanding and a good memory.

There were, in the persons of some of the dons at Oxford and Cambridge in the late Victorian and Edwardian periods, a group of Platonic guardians. Some approached, but of course seldom achieved, the perfect qualities of Plato's True Guardians, some resembled Auxiliaries, and most were a nineteenth and twentieth century composite of the Platonic ideal and of period fashion.

Contemporaneous with these dons, and parallel to the emergence of Heyck's intellectual,[68] existed an undergraduate and collegiate fashion – athleticism. This phenomenon at the ancient universities has been too lightly dismissed, casually overlooked, even purposefully reduced. It does not, of course, accord with modern values, projections and aspirations. Yet it is to be guilty of casual or calculated neglect, I would suggest, to fail to grasp the essence of a past era and a system. There can be little doubt about athleticism's presence, popularity, and pervasiveness. It was strongly manifested in distinct and pronounced ways: in the striking change of topography; in the content of magazines; in the nature of *Valetes* and obituaries; in comment in subsequent biographies, autobiographies, memoirs and reminiscences; in critical and supportive commentaries; in the organisational arrangement of colleges; and in the qualifications required for careers (especially in teaching and in the imperial service). Last but not least, it showed itself in the period preferences, enthusiasms and activities of a number of dons. This is symbolised, perhaps, by the story G. B. Grundy recounted of an Oxford walk in the mid-nineties with the epicurean Walter Pater.

One day when we were going along the path under Merton wall, I noticed that the then newly founded dons' hockey club was playing on the meadow by the side of it. It attracted Pater's attention, and he said to me, 'Who are these, playing on this field? I did not know games were allowed there.' I told him it was the new don's hockey club. He looked at it for a moment and then took my arm and said, 'Come away, I don't think we ought to look.' . . . It was the expression of his sense of the indecency involved in middle-aged Fellows of colleges engaging in such a pastime. As a fact, 'pastime' is too mild a word to apply to it. It was the most dangerous game I ever saw, and I had played football in former years for Blackheath, a notoriously large-sized and rough team . . . But this game on Merton Meadow played by many who had never before taken violent exercise resulted in far more casualties, so that those who participated in it might be distinguished by black eyes, scars, bandages, and sticking plaster. They played regardless of the laws of God, especially as illustrated by the sixth commandment, or those of man, or those of hockey.[69]

These men were, of course, simply dons caught up in the fashion and passions of the time. Like the Morgans at Jesus College, of whom I have written elsewhere,[70] these men, in varying degrees, embodied a new morality and epitomised a new pedagogic ideal. They were moral tutors as much as, and sometimes in preference to, scholastic intellectuals. They were, of course, of many inclinations and mixtures of inclinations – realists, casuists, idealists and pragmatists, but all subscribed to the period educational shibboleth: character training, if not exclusively then substantially, through athletic activity. Even as late as the 1920s, T. E. B. Howarth could write of Cambridge: 'There was no lack of emphasis on the purifying and ennobling quality of team sports as an agent of moral rectitude.' As with the 'beaks' in the public schools, the endorsing and supporting dons were human-values filters, focusing mechanisms and mnemonic agents.[71] For these reasons their attitude and behaviour, as well as those of the students, should be recorded, scrutinised and analysed. Only in this way will an accurate and complete social history of these famous universities be written, and incidentally, only in this way will Kearney's complaint about official university histories be rectified.

Notes

1. Hugh Kearney, *Scholars and Gentlemen: Universities and Society in Pre-industrial Britain, 1500–1700* (London, 1970) Introduction, p. 1.
2. T. B. Howarth, *Cambridge Between Two Wars* (London, 1978) pp. 16–17.
3. For a brief discussion of this phenomenon see J. A. Mangan, *Athleticism in the Victorian and Edwardian Public School: the emergency of consolidation of an educational ideology* (Cambridge, 1981) pp. 122–127. The

author is completing a fuller study to be entitled *Liberal Education, The Ancient Universities and the Games Ethic.*

4. 'Oars and the Man: Pleasure and Purpose in Victorian and Edwardian Cambridge', *History of Higher Education Annual*, 1984, pp. 52–77.
5. W. W. Rouse-Ball, *Cambridge Notes* (Cambridge, 1921) pp. 105–106.
6. W. H. Spooner, 'Fifty Years in an Oxford College', unpublished autobiographical notes, New College Archives, p. 64.
7. 'Classical Education at Cambridge', *Cambridge Review*, 23 November 1893, p. 110.
8. 'The Mind and the Body', *Spectator*, May 1886.
9. *Granta*, vol. XI, no. 231, 5 March 1898, p. 226.
10. 'As Others See Us', *Cambridge Review*, vol. XXIII, no. 582, 24 April 1902, p. 266.
11. Hans E. von Lindeiner-Wildan, 'A Rhodes Scholar from Germany', *The Cornhill Magazine*, vol. XVIII, no. 103, NS, 1905, pp. 47–48.
12. 'Magister Regens', *Oxford and Cambridge Review* no. 15, July 1911, p. 171.
13. *Granta*, vol. XVIII, no. 393, 18 February 1905, p. 174.
14. *Isis*, 23 February 1895, pp. 191–2.
15. *Granta*, vol. III, no. 26, 25 January 1890, p. 1.
16. Frank Rutter, *Varsity Types: Scenes and Characters from Undergraduate Life* (Cambridge, 1911).
17. Rowland Prothero, *Whippingham to Westminster* (London, 1938) p. 43.
18. J. A. Mangan, *Athleticism*, p. 122. The expression is Noel Annan's.
19. *Gownsman*, vol. II, no. 43, 6 May 1911, p. 550.
20. *Granta*, vol. IV, no. 54, May 1891, p. 9
21. 'Those in Authority', *Granta*, vol. II, no. 4, 8 February 1889, p. 10.
22. See for example a particularly interesting set of idols in vols XIII and XIV between March 1899 and June 1899: Mr Morris Nickalls, 18 March 1899, p. 232, Mr Charles Evelyn Johnston, 6 May 1899, p. 264, Mr Howard R. Parkes, 27 May 1899, p. 310 and Mr Cecil F. J. Holmes, 3 June 1899, p. 322.
23. Sheldon Rothblatt, *The Revolution of the Dons* (Cambridge, 1981) (2nd Ed.).
24. E. H. Craddock, Brasenose College BA 1881, BD & DD 1854, Fellow of Brasenose to 1845, Principal 1853 to 1886. See Fred. Boase, *Modern English Biography*, vol. 1 (London, 1965) pp. 746–7.
25. *Granta*, vol. III, no. 17, 18 October 1889, p. 10.
26. F. W. Bussell, 'The Old System of Education', *Oxford and Cambridge Review*, no. 15, July 1911, pp. 120–142.
27. G. M. Edwards, *Pheon*, Tercentenary Edition, 14 February 1896, p. 27.
28. 'Tea Time: An Elegy', *Griffin*, vol. II, no. 2, Lent Term, 1905, p. 13.
29. 'The Plaint of the Ancient Don', *Lady Clare Magazine*, vol. 1, no. 16, 9 June 1898, p. 8.
30. Reminiscences of E. C. M. *Lincoln Imp*, no. 9, Hilary Term, 1946, p. 29.
31. *Granta*, vol. IX, no. 177, 1 February 1896, p. 157.
32. From *The Undergraduate or a College Life in five phases. A Satire by B. A. Cantab* quoted in *Cambridge Review*, vol. VII, no. 158, 4 November 1885, p. 64.

33. *Granta*, vol. VII, no. 121, 11 November 1893, pp. 77–78.
34. *Granta*, vol. X, no. 200, 23 January 1897, p. 132.
35. 'At a Lecture' *Oxford Magazine*, vol. XXIII, no. 19, 17 May 1905, p. 319.
36. 'Song of the Lecture Room', *Cambridge Review*, 13 May 1909, p. 384.
37. Editorial in *Granta*, vol. X, no. 194, 31 October 1896, pp. 31–32.
38. 'The Mere Don', *Granta*, vol. X, no. 193, 24 October 1896, pp. 27–29.
39. Editorial, *Isis*, no. 168, 18 March 1899, p. 230.
40. '"My Tutor", By a Cynical Undergraduate', *Granta*, vol. IX, no. 144, 7 December 1895, verses 4 and 5, p. 18.
41. *Granta*, vol. XI, no. 224, 22 January 1898, p. 17.
42. Michael Holroyd, *Lytton Strachey* (Harmondsworth, 1987) p. 177.
43. *Silver Crescent*, no. 31, June 1901, pp. 27–28.
44. 'Divine Songs for Men' by K, *Granta*, vol. X, no. 209, 1 May 1897, p. 288.
45. 'Eureka' by R. G., *Oxford Magazine*, vol. XIX, no. 6, 21 November 1890, p. 99.
46. *Granta*, vol. IV, no. 51, 24 January 1891, p. 192.
47. *Oxford Review*, 21 January 1885, p. 72.
48. Ibid., p. 75
49. *Lady Clare Magazine*, vol. II, no. 2, May Term, 1903, p. 21.
50. Editorial, *Griffin*, vol. II, no. 2, Lent Term, 1905, p. 2.
51. *Lady Clare Magazine*, vol. III, no. 1, October Term, 1903, p. 20.
52. *Lady Clare Magazine*, vol. VI, no. 3, Easter Term, 1907, pp. 17 and 36.
53. Ibid., p. 36.
54. Richard Bird, *The Laggard in Love: An Improbable Comedy* (1911).
55. Gertrude Himmelfarb, *Victorian Minds* (London, 1968) pp. 202ff.
56. Ibid., p. 203.
57. *Silver Crescent*, no. 35, December 1902, p. 1.
58. H. E. Malden, 'The Master of Trinity Hall', *Cambridge Review*, vol. XXIV, no. 590, 16 October 1902, p. 6.
59. Ibid., p. 7.
60. Ibid., p. 8.
61. 'A Sermon preached in the Chapel of Trinity Hall on March 13th, 1870', Cambridge University Archives, Cam. C8870, 36.
62. *Cambridge Review*, vol. XXIV, no. 591, 23 October 1902, p. 22.
63. See 'In Memoriam William Teuton Swan Stallybrass', *Brazen Nose*, vol IX, no. 1, May 1949, pp. 9–26.
64. Memories of B. L. Jones, *Brazen Nose*, vol. III, no. 5, November 1921, p. 255.
65. See *Brazen Nose*, vol. III, no. 1, November 1919, p. 23.
66. Obituary of Charles Taylor, *Eagle*, vol. III, October Term, 1908, p. 84.
67. Ibid., p. 84.
68. See T. A. Heyck, *The Transformation of intellectual life in Victorian England* (London, 1982).
69. G. B. Grundy, *Fifty five Years at Oxford: an unconventional autobiography* (London, 1945).
70. See Mangan 'Oars and the Man', pp. 60–66.
71. Howarth, *Cambridge Between Two Wars*, p. 58.

Index

Abrahams, A, 101, 103
Abrahams, H, 6, 11, 99–107
Abrahams, S, 101, 103
Acestes, 15, 20–2
Achilles, 14–17, 21, 24, 25
Adrastus, 23–4
Addison, 89
Aeneas, 14–16, 19–21, 25
Aeschylus, 4
Aesop, 8
Agamemnon, 21
Aias, 18, 19, 21, 25
Alcidamas, 23
Almond, H, 10, 116, 119–20, 126, 128
Alston, R, 101, 103, 107
Anchises, 14
Antilochos, 17
Archery, 5, 15, 19, 21
Argylleus, 23
Aristotle, 3–4, 86, 88
Arlott, J, 17, 18
Armitage, J, 69
Arnold, M, 31–2, 38, 43, 45, 47–8, 50, 111, 117, 127, 132
Arnold, T, 10, 112–13, 126, 132
Ascanius, 15
Asquith, R, 125
Athene, 17–18, 102
Athens, 10, 109–10, 119
Augustus, 15
Austen, J, 66

Bacon, 133
Bainbridge, P, 131
Banking, 53–4, 58
Bathing, 9, 73, 79, 113
Baynes, D, 131
Baudelaire, 40, 42, 50
Beech, 7, 56–7
Beerbohm, 6
Beethoven, 4
Bell, C, 35–8

Bellini, 72
Belloc, H, 7, 64, 67
Berkeley, 3
Bible, 3, 4
Bird, R, 146
Blackwell, T, 27, 37
Blake, 6, 29–31, 38
Blandings Castle, 8, 56–7, 59
Bloomsbury, 6, 32, 34–7
Boaden, J, 91, 98
Boccaccio, 3
Bohemia, 32, 37
Botticelli, 72
Boucher, 74, 79
Bowen, E, 117, 127–8
Boxing, 5, 12, 15, 16, 23, 53–5, 65, 115
Boydell, J, 88, 97
Brasenose College, Oxford, 137–8, 143, 146, 153
Breughel, 11, 73, 79
Britten, 12
Brooke, R, 125
Brown, J, 28, 37
Browning, 32–4, 111
Buchan, J, 123–4, 129
Bussell, F, 137–8, 143, 146, 153
Byron, 44

Caesar, 15, 141
Caius College, Cambridge, 99, 101
Cambridge, 10, 11, 18, 99, 101, 103, 111, 130–54
Cambridge Review, 141, 147, 153
Capaneus, 23
Carlyle, 111
Carroll, 8, 17, 47
Carter, G, 90
Catiline, 16
Catullus, 71
Censors hip, 82, 84
Cézanne, 77–8
Chardin, 2